Bicycling
the Pioneer Valley
... and Beyond

*28 Scenic Road Bike Tours
in the Connecticut River Valley Region
of Western Massachusetts*

by Marion Gorham

New England Cartographics
North Amherst, Massachusetts
1998

D0684577

Copyright © 1998 by Marion Gorham

Published by New England Cartographics, Inc.

New England Cartographics
P.O. Box 9369, North Amherst MA 01059

Cover design by Bruce Scofield
Maps by Montague Mapping
Photographs by Al Shane, Marion Gorham & Bruce Scofield
Text editing and layout by Valerie Vaughan

Publishers Cataloging in Publication

Gorham, Marion
    Bicycling the Pioneer Valley ... and beyond: 28 scenic
    road bike tours in the Connecticut River Valley region of
    Western Massachusetts / by Marion Gorham.
    176 p. Includes maps.
    ISBN 1-889787-02-7   LC 98-66238
    1. Bicycling. 2. Bicycle paths -- New England. I. Title.
    796.6 -- dc20

Due to changes in trail and road conditions, the use of information in this book is at the sole risk of the user.

Printed in the United States of America
10 9 8 7 6 5 4 3 2 1   02 01 00 99 98

Acknowledgments

This book began when Chris Ryan, owner of New England Cartographics, asked my husband Al and me to write a book on bicycling in the Pioneer Valley. Although Al declined, he encouraged me to go ahead and he helped me with all but the actual writing. I like to write; he doesn't. We both like to ride.

We have been serious bicyclists since the late 1960s when we first met. A month-long bicycle-camping tour of Nova Scotia and Newfoundland cemented our relationship and has led to touring in Ireland, Scotland, England, Wales, Germany, Austria, Norway, the Czech Republic and Canadian Rockies, as well as in this country, including Alaska. All of these trips have been wonderful, but we feel that bicycling in the Pioneer Valley is "as good as it gets."

In this book we share some of our favorite rides with you. Some are originals and some were designed by members of local bicycle clubs, the Franklin-Hampshire Freewheelers or the Springfield Cyclonauts. I would like to thank members of these clubs, especially Bob Kowaleski, Don Maynard, Joanne Nadolny, Sally Peters, Ken and Irene Sherman, Jerry Weinstein, and Michael Bosworth of Montague Mapping. Of course, I would also like to thank my publisher, Chris Ryan, for asking me to write this book, and Valerie Vaughan, who edited the text. It really was fun to create new rides and to ride the old familiar ones, describing and reliving them in the process. Most of all, I want to thank my husband, Albert Shane, without whom I could not have written this book. He rode the rides with me, advised and encouraged me. He read the mileage at turns and points of interest so I could jot them down as we rode along on our tandem. Some of the rides listed here are his rides. For all this and more: Thank you, Al.

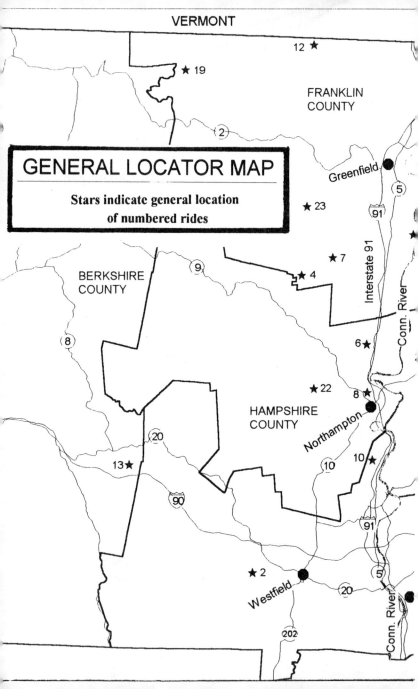

GENERAL LOCATOR MAP

Stars indicate general location of numbered rides

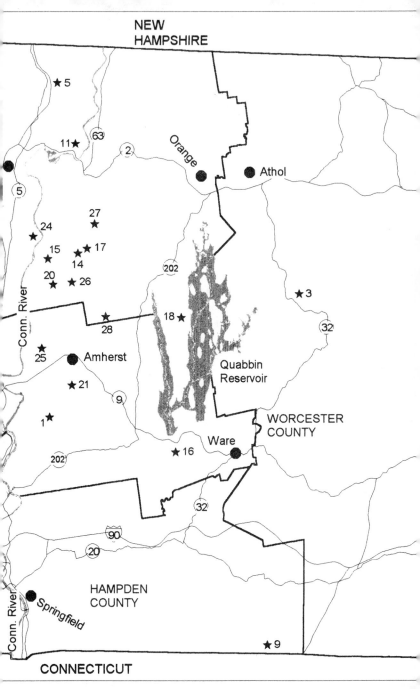

Contents

Introduction

This book contains rides in and around the Pioneer Valley of western Massachusetts. The rides are scenic and versatile. They can be shortened, lengthened, and combined or connected with each other. Length, terrain, and level of difficulty vary. There is something for everyone here, and almost anyone can manage a portion of each ride. This guide lists designated starting points, but each ride can be started and finished anywhere along the described route. Rides can also be done in reverse. The possibilities are almost endless.

With its country roads, variable terrain, and pastoral scenery, the Pioneer Valley offers some of the best bicycling anywhere in the United States. Since it is located in a river valley, there is enough flat terrain to suit beginners and novices, but there are also hills to be climbed by the more experienced cyclists. Few of the hills are really steep; most are rolling (gentle), but this is relative to the experience and physical strength of each cyclist.

The rides listed here have been rated as *novice, intermediate* or *advanced*. They might have been called easy, moderate or difficult. These are relative terms, depending on the riders' ability and experience, as well as other factors. What might be a difficult ride in the spring could be considered an easy ride in the fall. Because the local environment is excellent for bicycling, the Pioneer Valley has been a very popular site for bicycle rallies, such as the New England Area Rally in 1985, the Eastern Tandem Rally in 1990, and the Great Eastern Rally in 1995. These rallies were all centered at the University of Massachusetts in Amherst. Such rallies are sponsored by local clubs in cooperation with national or regional organizations such as the League of American Bicyclists and the Tandem Club of America, attracting hundreds of cyclists to the area.

The Pioneer Valley is home to two bicycle touring clubs: the Franklin-Hampshire Freewheelers and the Springfield Cyclonauts Bicycling Club. Many of the rides in this book are derived from these club and rally rides. The reader is cautioned that, although all roads used in these rides were rideable at the time of publication, road conditions can change. Roads are artificial impositions on the environment and are subject to natural cycles as well as human intervention. While some roads may have deteriorated during winter storms and spring melts, others may have been improved by new pavement. A smooth, hard-surfaced gravel road can be easier riding than a paved road with pot-holes and loose gravel. Because road conditions can be variable and inconsistent, the reader is advised in general to be careful and to expect the unexpected.

How to Use This Book

After reading all the introductory sections, take a preliminary look at the rides. Select one based on your ability and interest. It is best to read through the description and all the directions (including alternatives) *completely* before starting your ride. In addition to packing this book with your other gear, you may want to make an abbreviated cue sheet from the directions and put it in the map case on your handlebar bag or clip it to the handlebars. Use the milepoints to give you an approximation of when to turn. Cyclometers do not always record the same mileage; they sometimes need adjusting. Street signs can sometimes disappear, street names can change, and roadmaps are not always accurate.

If a ride looks interesting but is longer or more hilly than you desire, consider riding a part of it and backtracking, or try spotting cars, a technique popular with hikers and canoeists. Two cars are driven to whatever point you wish to complete the ride, where one car is parked. The second car is then used to return the driver of the parked car back to the ride start. If only two persons are involved, both cars should have the ability to carry bicycles. If more than two persons are involved, the bicycles may be dropped off at the ride start with a third person (or more) to await the return of the car spotters. At the end of the ride the spotted car returns the driver or drivers to the ride start.

Safety and Courtesy

In Massachusetts the bicycle is legally classified as a vehicle, which means that the same laws that apply to cars apply to bicycles -- stopping at stop signs, using directional signals (your hand), riding on the right-hand side of the road and, as a slow-moving vehicle, riding to the far right if it is safe. It is not safe to ride on loose gravel, pot-holes, or soft shoulders, and it is not safe to ride to the far right if you are going to make a left turn.

Cyclists should ride single file except to pass and should pull off the road onto the shoulder whenever they stop. It is vital to keep the bicycle under control at all times, especially when going downhill, to exercise care on blind curves, and to watch for hazards such as loose gravel, potholes, dogs, and open car doors. Railroad tracks should be crossed at a right angle to avoid entrapping the wheel and throwing the rider. Directions in this book will include warnings about railroad tracks. Read the directions thoroughly before starting the ride so that you will be prepared.

Equipment

For road-biking a touring bike is best. Mountain bikes are O.K. but their fat tires offer more road resistance than touring bike tires, thus making for a slower ride. Also, their handle bars do not offer the variety of positions which drop handle bars offer unless bar extensions are used. Hands can become numb if held in the same position too long and can become temporarily paralyzed. The hybrid bicycle falls somewhere in between the mountain bike and the touring bike. Racing bikes may be acceptable, but their gearing is too high for hills and their tires too skinny for gravel roads.

Your bicycle should fit you. The size of the bicycle, height of the top tube, height of the seat, and the reach are all important for a comfortable ride. Have your bicycle adjusted to you by a knowledgeable dealer or salesperson, who is a cyclist and has a good repair service. Good maintenance is essential.

Essential equipment:

1. An approved helmet worn properly; i.e., covering the forehead. Straps should be properly adjusted and snug; they may have to be adjusted frequently.
2. Spare tube or patch kit. Know how to use them.
3. Bicycle pump, attached to bike.
4. Water bottle holder(s) and water bottle(s) -- filled.
5. Handlebar bag with map case or handlebar clip attachment for map or cue sheet
6. Tire irons to assist in changing tire
7. Sturdy bicycle lock
8. Bright colored clothing (for visibility)
9. Front and rear lights if you plan to ride at night
10. Reflectors

Other recommended equipment:

1. Bicycle gloves or grab-ons (or both)
2. Padded shorts (for comfort)
3. Fenders (to prevent a muddy streak up your back when caught in the rain)
4. Backrack for attaching a rackpack or pannier bags, or strapping extra clothing to the back of the bike.

5. Rack duffel, panniers, hold-down straps
6. Cyclocomputer (for recording mileage and using with cue sheets)
7. Compass
8. A road map is very helpful if you go off the route either accidentally or intentionally. County and real estate maps give street names. For a listing of useful maps, see page 169.

Bicycle stores and catalogs can give further information about equipment and clothing. Local bicycle stores are listed on page 172.

Technique

Know how to use your gears. Use high gears on flat terrain, low gears for the hills. Anticipate the need to shift gears and shift *before* the going gets tough.

Brake carefully. Use rear (right-hand) brake first. Too sudden braking or braking with front (left-hand) brake first can throw you over the handle bars.

Pace yourself. Start out at a reasonable pace. Increase your pace as you go along. Rest as needed. Its O.K. to walk up a hill or part of a hill.

Drink plenty of fluids; don't let yourself become dehydrated. Water is the best fluid. Avoid alcohol. Snack as needed.

Enjoy the scenery. Smell the flowers. Stop to enjoy a view. Visit a site of interest. Enjoy the ride. Go for the aesthetics as well as the athletics.

Bicycle Clubs and Organizations

Bicycle clubs sponsor weekend rides and other activities. Organizations sponsor rallies and provide services to individuals and clubs. Both clubs and organizations provide newsletters or magazines and schedules of activities. Consult the listing on page 170 for names, addresses and telephone numbers of area bicycle clubs and national organizations.

To ride with a club the cyclist should be able to ride a distance of twenty (preferably thirty) miles at a minimal speed of twelve miles per hour. Most club cyclists ride 15-to-16 mph, which can be discouraging for beginning riders, who get left in the dust. However, maps or cue sheets are generally provided and all cyclists ride at their own pace; designated regroups allow the slower riders to catch up. Sometimes a sweep is appointed in addition to a leader.

Riders are responsible for their own safety and well-being and may be required to sign a statement to this effect. Helmets are required and riders should carry water bottles, spare tubes, or patch kits and snacks. They should be prepared to repair their own flat tires and have someone to call if they are unable to complete the ride.

In addition to rides, clubs may organize picnics, potlucks and off-season activities, as well as an annual meeting and a banquet. Clubs may also schedule mountain bike rides for those who enjoy this popular variation.

Ride Starts

The rides in this book start at areas that have sufficient parking for several vehicles, but they can be started anywhere along the route where one or two vehicles can be parked. The Mill River Recreation Area in North Amherst, the Mount Sugarloaf Parking Area in South Deerfield and the parking area behind the Hadley Village Barn Shops in Hadley are popular ride starts with the Franklin-Hampshire Freewheelers. The Cyclonauts rides generally start from the ride leaders' homes or from parking areas in the Springfield area. We encourage you to start wherever you like, but park well off the road.

Advice to Beginners

Beginners are advised to take short rides around their own neighborhood before attempting longer rides. You will know when you are ready for longer rides when you find that your neighborhood is expanding. It is possible to expand the length of your routes from five to 100 miles within a year.

The Norwottuck Rail Trail and the Northampton Bike Path are appropriate for beginners because they are flat and free of automobile traffic except for road crossings. However, as soon as you are ready, expand your horizon, go for the open road and tackle some easy hills. Bicycle frequently. Get into shape and stay in shape - and have fun!

This introduction was not intended to be the final word on bicycling. Whole books have been written on technique, equipment, and bicycle maintenance, and some of these are listed in the *References*, page 167. Bicycle magazines also contain more detail on these areas.

1

Around the Range

Rating: Intermediate
Distance: 19, 27, 29 or 37 miles
Terrain: Flat to hilly
Towns: Amherst, Hadley, South Hadley, Granby, Belchertown

Points of Interest: Porter-Phelps-Huntington House, Hadley Farm Museum, Hadley Flea Market, Mount Holyoke Range, Skinner State Park, Flood Marker, South Hadley Village Commons, Mt. Holyoke College, Atkins Farms Country Market, Hadley Farm, and the University of Massachusetts.

Description: The complete 37-mile ride starts from North Amherst, but shorter rides may be started from Hadley or South Amherst. The ride may also be shortened en route. All routes go around the Mount Holyoke Range and provide excellent views of the range and the historic Summit House. The first 12 miles of the complete route are relatively flat, with the route traveling through farmland, rural residential areas, and along the Connecticut River. The hills that come later on are gradual, not steep, but can be annoying if you don't like climbing. Walking is always an alternative. The end of the ride is flat.

Ride at your own pace, stop when you like, and enjoy the scenery. There are tobacco fields, corn fields, potato fields, pumpkin patches, and strawberry fields, where you can pick your own strawberries (in season). In late February and early March, which can be good bicycling on a warm day, sap buckets appear on the trees and the North Hadley Sugar

Shack invites visitors. In the fall, vegetable and fruit stands pop out along the wayside. With all these diversions you might never complete the ride, but there's always another day. The two refreshment stops listed here are favorites with bicyclists and are conveniently timed along this ride. They offer good food, clean rest rooms, indoor and outdoor tables.

OPTIONS: For a shorter ride, start at the Village Barn Shops on Route 9 in Hadley (mile 7.9 in directions below). Park in back of the shops, go left on Bay Road, straight on Route 47, and follow the directions to South Hadley and around the range to Atkins Country Market. After stopping at Atkins, continue on West Bay Road past South Maple Street (mile 30.3), right on Route 47, and left on Bay Road to the Village Barn Shops. This shortens the ride by 10 miles. Another option written into the directions shortens it another eight.

An even shorter ride can be started at Atkins Country Market in South Amherst. Go left on West Bay Rd., then left on Rte. 47 to South Hadley, following the route of the longer ride and continue on that route back to Atkins Country Market. For the longer ride, begin at the Mill River Recreation Area in North Amherst.

Directions:
START at the Mill River Recreation Area on Rte. 63 in North Amherst. A small sign on two posts indicates the driveway leading to the parking lots. There are restrooms on both sides of the park building.
0.0 LEFT on Rte. 63. Go past the Riverside Park Shops.
0.2 CROSS OVER to Old Sunderland Rd. and take a RIGHT at the lights onto Meadow St.
0.6 CROSS Rte. 116 and continue on Meadow St.
0.8 RIGHT on Russellville Rd., which becomes Comins Rd. in Hadley. Enjoy this flat scenic stretch of farmland.

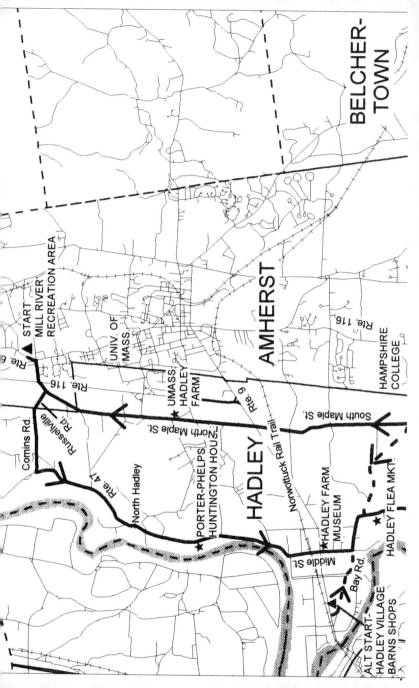

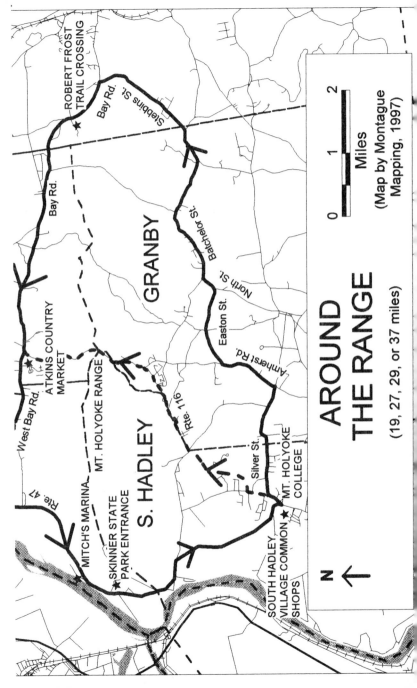

AROUND THE RANGE

(19, 27, 29, or 37 miles)

Map by Montague Mapping, 1997

Miles
0   1   2

N

ROBERT FROST TRAIL CROSSING

Bay Rd.

Stebbins St.

Bay Rd.

GRANBY

Batchelor St.

North St.

Easton St.

Amherst Rd.

ATKINS COUNTRY MARKET

West Bay Rd.

MT. HOLYOKE RANGE

Rte. 116

S. HADLEY

Rte. 47

MITCH'S MARINA

SKINNER STATE PARK ENTRANCE

Silver St.

MT. HOLYOKE COLLEGE

SOUTH HADLEY VILLAGE COMMON SHOPS

2.1 LEFT on Route 47 along the Connecticut River (sometimes in view), past scenic farms selling fruit, flowers and vegetables in season.

3.8 Ride slowly through the village of North Hadley. Lake Warner, on your left, was made by damming the same Mill River that flows through the Mill River Recreation Area in North Amherst. Read the plaque on the rock on your left for historic information.

5.3 The Porter-Phelps-Huntington House Historic House Museum is set back from the road on your right. Teas, tours and concerts are held here during the summer. The house dates back to 1752 and contains original furnishings and historic documents.

7.1 The Norwottuck Rail Trail crosses Route 47 (Middle Street). Gracious homes line both sides of the road as you approach Hadley center.

7.3 CROSS Route 9 at the lights and continue on Middle St. past the Hadley Town Hall. The Hadley Farm Museum is located behind the Town Hall and may be entered from Route 9. It displays antique farm implements and is free and open to the public.

7.9 LEFT at the T intersection at the end of Middle Street and continue on Route 47 south towards South Hadley. Note changing views of the Mount Holyoke range.

9.2 Hadley Flea Market (open in season) is on your right.

11.1 Mitch's Marina and Snack Bar are on your right.

11.3 The Flood Marker on your left indicates that your bike would have been under water during floods.

11.6 Skinner State Park entrance is on the left. Macho cyclists have been known to take a side trip to the summit. Forget it -- unless you really like climbing.

12.4 The road on the left (opposite the cemetery) offers access to the Metacomet-Monadnock hiking trail, which begins in Meriden, Connecticut and ends at Mount Monadnock in New Hampshire. One of its most beautiful sections is over the ridge of the Mount Holyoke range.

15.1 RIGHT at the Village Common Shops, noting the signs for the Odyssey Bookshop and Tailgate Picnic. Food and rest rooms should be welcome at this point, and the Tailgate has a great deli. Other restaurants are also located in this complex and Woodbridge's is in sight up the street. You may prefer to picnic on the town common just ahead on your right. Across the common is Mount Holyoke College, founded in 1837 by Mary Lyon. You may want to bike through the grounds and visit the greenhouse or the art museum.

15.2 LEFT on Route 116 from Rte. 47 or right from the College. (To shorten the ride, stay on 116 to Atkins Country Market and pick up the original route there. This option involves a long uphill, followed by a long downhill).

15.3 RIGHT on Silver St., a long gentle uphill.

16.4 BEAR LEFT where the road curves at the top of the hill.

17.3 LEFT on Amherst Road, mainly residential.

18.2 RIGHT on Easton St., rural.

19.6 LEFT on North St., also rural.

19.8 BEAR RIGHT on Batchelor Street (North St. flows into Batchelor).

22.0 LEFT at the T intersection to Stebbins St. (no sign)

24.4 LEFT on Bay Road

25.9 The Robert Frost Hiking Trail crosses the road here. This trail extends from the Mt. Holyoke Range in Amherst to the Mt. Toby Range in Sunderland and to Wendell State Forest in Wendell.

29.0 LEFT on Route 116

29.1 RIGHT on West Bay Road

29.2 LEFT into Atkins for a rest, refreshments and pit stop, then left onto West Bay Rd. again to continue the ride.

30.3 RIGHT on South Maple St. UMASS will be visible in the distance on your right as you bike through scenic farmlands, and the Berkshire hills will become visible in the distance on your left.

32.6 CROSS the Norwottuck Rail Trail. Watch for cyclists, skateboarders and pedestrians. Hampshire Mall will be on your right and Mountain Farms Mall on your left.

33.0 CROSS Route 9 to North Maple St. Farmland resumes here but development is encroaching.

34.0 CROSS Rocky Hill Road at the lights.

34.1 PASS the UMASS Hadley Farm on your right. Horses and sometimes sheep graze in the fields. The University is visible in the background. North Maple St. becomes Roosevelt St., which then becomes Meadow St.

36.7 CROSS Route 116 at the lights and continue on Meadow.

37.0 LEFT on Route 63 at the next set of lights, pass the Riverside Park Shops, cross the bridge over the Mill River and pass two houses.

37.3 RIGHT into the Mill River Recreation Area. If you feel up to it, you can now play a game of tennis, take a hike or a swim - or just flop on the grass and take a rest.

2

Cobble Mountain Reservoir

Rating: Intermediate to Advanced
Distance: 30 miles
Terrain: Flat to hilly
Towns: Westfield, Southwick, Granville, Blandford, Russell

Points of Interest: Stanley Park, Granville Gorge, Granville Country Store, Cobble Mt. Reservoir, Westfield State College.

Description: This ride is mainly flat until Route 57 when it becomes flat to rolling and continues flat to rolling until Wildcat Road, which is definitely hilly. After that it becomes flat and ends in a magnificent downhill. The route starts from Stanley Park in Westfield and proceeds into the countryside on lightly traveled roads through farmland and small towns, into the hills and back down again.

Stanley Park offers a great place to start and finish with an opportunity to enjoy a picnic after the ride and (if you time it right) a concert. This 100-acre park includes gardens, woodland trails, picnic areas, a dining pavilion and meeting house. Its focal point is a 96-foot gold-domed Carillon Tower with English and Flemish bells, an organ, stained glass windows, and sculptured bronze doors. In front of the tower is an inlaid slate map of the United States and Canada. In the pond area there is a replica of a Vermont covered bridge, a blacksmith shop, and a reconstructed mill from nearby Montgomery. A five-acre arboretum features a 30-foot illuminated fountain. Further attractions include dinosaur tracks, a totem pole, "enchanted oak," lily ponds with swans, a spectacular rose garden, and "The Prayer Boulder." Be sure to allow some time after the ride to enjoy the park.

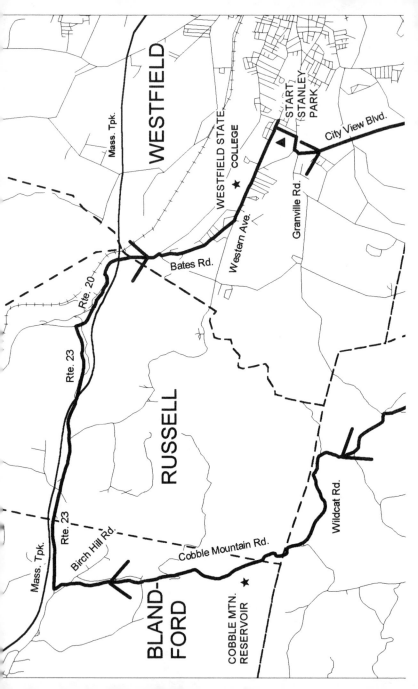

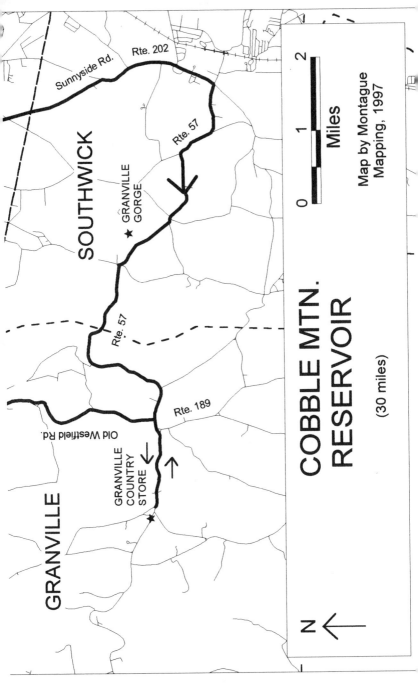

Westfield is the site of America's first bicycle factory, and the Columbia bicycle is still being produced there. Southwick, the next town en route, is a farming and lake resort community. It provides a last chance to buy food before Granville, a small town on top of a hill with an historic district and town common. The common is graced by a yellow brick library, white frame church, and a great little country store, which dates back to 1851 and is known for its cellar-aged cheese.

Along Cobble Mountain Reservoir in Blandford you will find a welcome respite from the hill-climbing. Stop at the spillway and look down into the gorge on your right as well as at the spillway on your left. Stop again on the bridge across the earth dam, which was the world's highest in 1931 when it was constructed, and enjoy the view of the Little River. Cobble Mountain Road leads out to Route 23, and then it's all downhill from there.

Directions:
START from Stanley Park on Western Ave. in Westfield.
    Park in the Japanese Garden parking area just inside the Main Gate (not the Recreational Gate, which is 0.3 miles north).
0.0 RIGHT onto Western Ave.
0.1 RIGHT on Kensington Ave., a lovely street that borders the park and passes the arboretum and the rhododendron display. It also passes two more entrances to the park (the second of which leads to restrooms near the picnic area).
0.5 RIGHT on Granville Rd.
0.6 CROSS over the bridge and go STRAIGHT onto City Blvd. There was no sign at the time of publication. This is a lovely country road, woodsy to residential. There's a very gradual uphill followed by a flat stretch and gentle downhill.
1.5 CROSS City View Rd.

2.4 STRAIGHT at the Stop sign onto Sunnyside Rd. You're in Southwick now and in farmland. The terrain continues to be flat to rolling.

3.3 Pass Sunnyside Farm on your right followed by a golf course on your left.

3.8 RIGHT on College Hwy., Rtes. 202 and 10. Pass Ray's Family Farm on your right. This stretch of road is interspersed with farmland, residential and commercial properties, including Noble Hospital Medical Affiliates. There are plenty of opportunities to eat or buy food.

5.6 RIGHT on Rte. 57 and leave the commercial stretch. An official Bike Route sign greets you as you make the turn. It will be uphill, interspersed with some flatness and downhill, all the way to Granville.

7.8 STRAIGHT and continue on Rte. 57 when the Bike Route goes off to the left.

9.0 Pass Grasshopper Greenery on your right.

9.2 Granville Gorge will be on your right. Watch for a trail that leads down to the water. Its worth taking a walk down and along the river. Continuing along the road, cliffs will appear on your left and the uphill will change to rolling terrain.

11.4 Granville Town Line

13.3 Pass Granville Village School on your left.

13.5 Pass Old Westfield Rd. on your right (you'll return to this later) and enter the Granville Historic District proclaimed by a sign.

13.7 LEFT at the junction with Rte. 189 and past the yellow brick Granville Public Library. At the white frame Granville Federated Church, bear right to the Granville Country Store. Pause here for food and rest before reversing your route past the church and library and taking a right on Rte. 57.

14.1 LEFT on Old Westfield Rd., which you passed earlier. The terrain is flat to rolling.

15.9 Pass Granville Reservoir, Westfield's water supply.

- 16.8 LEFT on Wildcat Rd. It's uphill and the blacktop may be a little patchy, but it's a pretty road, especially in June when the mountain laurel is in bloom. There are some rather impressive glacial erratic boulders on the right and you might see some wildlife.
- 19.6 LEFT at the triangle down to Cobble Mountain Reservoir and right on Cobble Mountain Rd., or go straight and you will come out on it anyhow.
- 19.9 Cross the Spillway, which will be on your left. The dam follows.
- 22.6 Suddenly there will be a house on your right, the first you've seen for a while. On your left there is what appears to be a beaver lodge in the middle of the meadow. Very shortly you will see the beaver pond with trees in standing water.
- 23.4 Cross Birch Hill Rd. and stay on Cobble Mountain Rd.
- 23.6 RIGHT on Rte. 23, which will be flat for a while.
- 24.6 Russell Town Line
- 26.6 CAUTION: Beginning of long, steep downhill. Maintain control of your bicycle! There's a turn at the bottom.
- 27.5 RIGHT on Rte. 20
- 29.3 RIGHT on Bates Rd.
- 30.5 Bates Rd. ends; Western Ave. begins.
- 30.8 Pass Westfield State College on your left.
- 31.8 RIGHT into the parking lot at Stanley Park. End of ride. The Japanese garden begins at the parking lot. Leave your bike and walk on through to enjoy the park.

3

Common to Common
and Store to Store

Rating: Intermediate
Distance: 40 miles
Terrain: Hilly
Towns: Petersham, Hardwick, Barre, Templeton, Philipston

Points of Interest: Petersham Common, Petersham Country Store, Hardwick Common, Hardwick General Store, Barre Common, Jackie's Country Kitchen, Templeton Common, Templeton Country Store and Templeton Ice Cream Barn

Description: Don't let the hills prevent you from doing this beautiful ride. You can always stop and rest, enjoy the peacefulness and beauty of the scenic country roads, or walk a bit. Since the route proceeds from Common to Common with stores or restaurants nearby, it is more like four short rides than one long one. However, because of the hills it is advisable to take this ride in comfortable weather. Ride at a leisurely pace, and bring along a lunch or buy food at one of the stores or restaurants. Commons are great for picnicking.

The route begins in a lovely residential area of Petersham (pronounced Peters-ham) and skirts the forested Quabbin Reservoir before arriving in Hardwick where the scenery changes to farmland and views of the neighboring hills. Barre is the largest town en route and it isn't big. However, it has a bicycle shop. Lightly traveled country roads, woods and fields, occasional ponds and lakes, as well as New England commons and country stores make this an interesting and enjoyable ride.

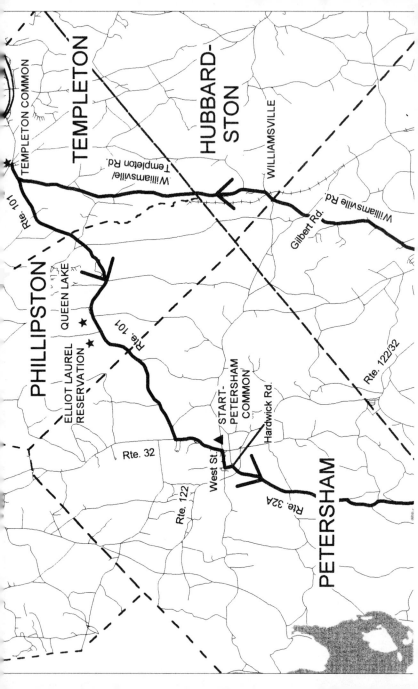

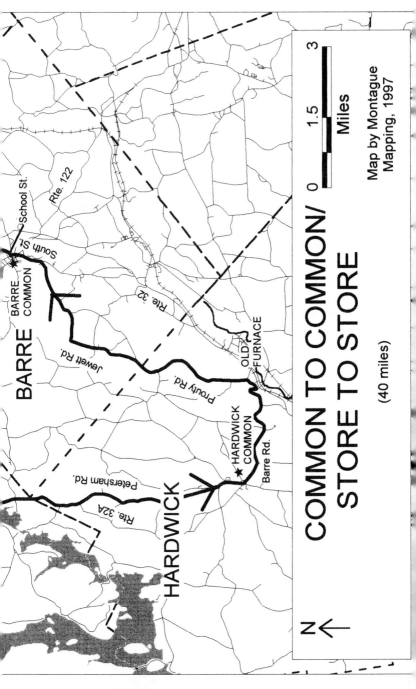

COMMON TO COMMON/
STORE TO STORE

(40 miles)

Map by Montague
Mapping, 1997

Miles

0   1.5   3

N

BARRE

BARRE COMMON

School St.
South St.
Rte. 122
Jewett Rd.
Rte. 32
Prouty Rd.
OLD FURNACE

HARDWICK

HARDWICK COMMON
Petersham Rd.
Rte. 32A
Barre Rd.

Directions:

START from the Petersham Common on South Main Street in Petersham near the Petersham Country Store, which has a restroom and small restaurant in the back.

0.0 RIGHT on West St. and past the Unitarian Church.

0.4 LEFT on Hardwick Rd. There's a large white house with pillars and black blinds on the corner.

0.6 BEAR RIGHT to stay on Hardwick Rd.

0.7 CROSS Rte. 122 and STRAIGHT on Rte. 32A and then downhill.

3.3 BEAR RIGHT to stay on 32A and continue downhill.

3.9 PASS Gate 40 to Quabbin Reservoir on your right; the road leads to the former town of Dana. Eventually, you will hit some uphill, but nothing to worry about.

5.7 CROSS Hardwick Town Line.

8.8 Observe the nice view on your right.

10.1 STRAIGHT onto Petersham Rd. as you approach Hardwick.

10.7 Hardwick Common will be on your left. Stop here or go on to the General Store.

10.8 LEFT on Barre Rd. in front of the Hardwick General Store and Post Office. Snack food and beverages are available and there's a toilet in the basement. The Calvin Paige Memorial opposite the store is a good place to sit and snack or there's a bench set further back on the Common. Next to the store is the Calvinist Congregational Church, and a short way down the road on your left is the Daniel Ruggles Tavern, dated 1809. Shortly, you will find yourself in farm country and rolling hills. After a long downhill with a curve to the right, BE PREPARED for a left turn uphill.

13.4 LEFT on Prouty Rd. and a short uphill. You're in the village of Old Furnace.

13.5 On your right in a cage are a pheasant and a peacock. In the adjoining field you may see calves, goats and llamas.

13.7 BEAR LEFT and stay on Prouty Rd. There are beautiful views on the left, but watch out for an attack turkey at a farm up the road. Further along, a mannequin sits on a tractor while a scarecrow stands in the garden. And at Maple Hill Farm there's a bear on the roof of a barn! The road flattens out here.

17.6 STOP SIGN! Four corners. Cross the road and go straight on Jewett St. Downhill will follow.

18.7 There's an interesting cemetery on the left, followed by a pretty little pond.

20.2 LEFT on South St. at the T intersection

20.5 Pass Cooks Canyon, a property of the Massachusetts Audubon Society.

20.7 Barre Common is on your left. On your right across the way is Jackie's Country Kitchen, offering ice cream, grinders, muffins and more. On a side street behind you there's a Cumberland Farms, the Barre Pizza Restaurant and Honey Farms Mini-Market. *OPTION:* A shortcut back to Petersham on Rtes. 32 and 122 from the middle of the Common (this shortcut is 8 miles long).

20.9 RIGHT on School St. after Country Bike & Sports Store and downhill and STRAIGHT onto Williamsville Rd. and uphill. It's not for long, however, and at the top you're out in the country again.

22.5 STRAIGHT to left to stay on Williamsville Rd. A flat stretch is followed by a downhill. CROSS Gilbert Rd.

25.0 BEAR LEFT on Williamsville-Templeton Rd. Pass the small white frame Williamsville Chapel on your right (dated 1888).

25.5 A lovely pond follows on the left.

30.6 RIGHT ON 101 uphill to a T intersection.

31.0 The Templeton Common will be on your left. For refreshments, go right to the Templeton Country Store or just past it to the Templeton Ice Cream Barn, a restaurant with a restroom.

31.0 REVERSE DIRECTION and go south on Rte. 101 down the hill you just came up. Careful, it is a bit bumpy. 101 has lots of ups and downs but the ride will end on a down.

33.3 CROSS the Philipston Town Line. There will be a pretty pond on the right.

34.8 Queen Lake, with its sandy beach, will be on the right.

35.2 Elliot Laurel Reservation, a 33-acre property of the Trustees of Reservations, will be on your right. A trail leads through the laurels and a hardwood forest to a hill with a view. The Philipston Wildlife Management Area will follow on the left.

36.8 Cross the Petersham Town Line.

39.1 LEFT on Rte. 32 and downhill.

39.7 Petersham Craft Center will be on your right. It is open Tues.-Sun. 11:30-4:00.

39.8 Pass North Common Meadows, another property of the Trustees of Reservations.

40.1 Petersham Common revisited; Petersham Country Store is awaiting a visit. End of an uncommonly good ride.

4

D.A.R. State Forest

Rating: Intermediate
Distance: 25 miles
Terrain: Hilly
Towns: Williamsburg, Conway, Ashfield, Goshen

Points of Interest: Chapelbrook Reservation, D.A.R. State Forest, Williamsburg General Store

Description: This ride is hilly but manageable, the scenery is outstanding and, best of all, it ends with a long downhill all the way into Williamsburg. The first portion of the ride follows the route of *Going to the Chapel* (Ride 7) and passes by Chapelbrook Reservation where you can view a part of Chapel Falls from the road. For more details about Chapelbrook Reservation, refer to the description in *Going to the Chapel.*

The second part of this ride goes west on Creamery Road in Ashfield to Route 112 and south to D.A.R. State Forest, which is the focal point of the ride. Drinking water, picnic tables, restrooms, swimming, canoeing, camping, and hiking are all available. Pick up a map of the trails so you can come back another time to hike or cross-country ski.

From D.A.R., the route continues through the forest to Ludwig Road, which leads to Williamsburg Road and a long downhill which makes the uphill worthwhile. Another reward awaits you at the end of the ride. The Williamsburg General Store has ice cream, coffee and pastry.

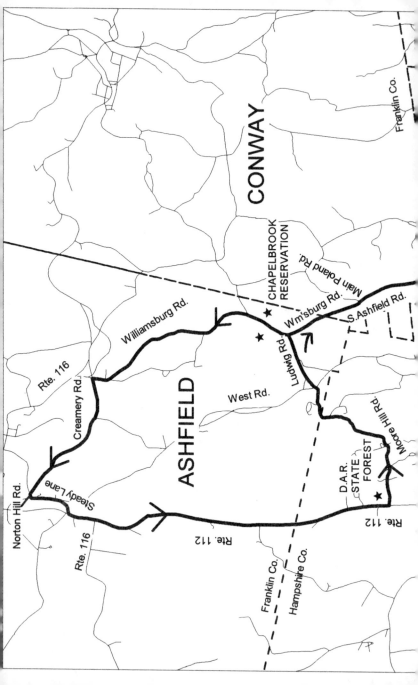

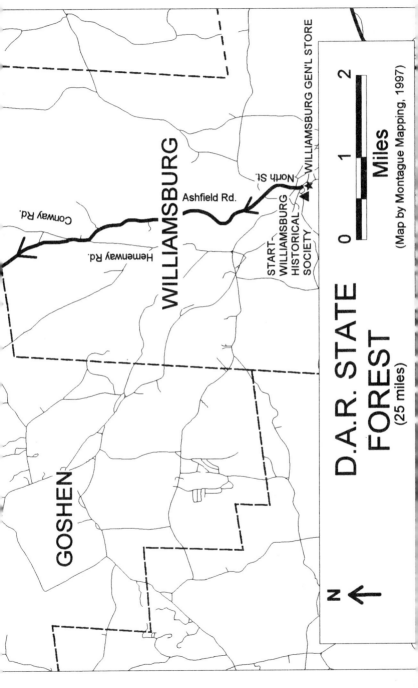

D.A.R. STATE FOREST
(25 miles)

GOSHEN

WILLIAMSBURG

Conway Rd.

Hemenway Rd.

Ashfield Rd.

North St.

START —
WILLIAMSBURG
HISTORICAL
SOCIETY

WILLIAMSBURG GEN'L STORE

Miles

0   1   2

(Map by Montague Mapping, 1997)

N

Directions:

START from the parking area behind the Williamsburg
  Historical Society and the Historic Williams
  Restaurant on Rte. 9 in Williamsburg. Enter the
  parking area by the driveway between the Williamsburg
  Grange and the Historical Society or via South St.

0.0 LEFT on Rte. 9 from the above driveway.

0.1 BEAR RIGHT onto North St., cross North Main and
  on North St. through a pleasant residential area.

0.5 North St. becomes Ashfield Rd. and the surroundings
  are rural.

3.2 BEAR LEFT and remain on Ashfield Rd. where it
  intersects with Conway Rd.

4.2 Conway Town Line. Here Ashfield Rd. becomes
  Williamsburg Rd.

5.3 Pass Main Poland Rd.

5.8 South Ashfield Town Line.

6.4 Pass Ludwig Rd. You will come out here near the end of
  the ride.

7.0 Chapelbrook Reservation. The path to Chapel Ledge will
  be on the left; Chapel Brook and Falls is on the right.

9.3 LEFT on Creamery Rd., which is a beautiful road along a
  brook, through woods, and past fields, farms, and
  beautiful homes.

10.9 Creamery Bridge Sugar House will be on your left over a
  small covered bridge.

11.1 LEFT on Norton Hill Rd. followed by an immediate left
  on Steady Lane.

11.7 LEFT on Rte. 112 South which alternates from flat to
  rolling all the way to D.A.R. State Forest

14.7 Goshen Town Line.

15.9 LEFT into D.A.R. State Forest just past a State Forest
  road sign.

16.2 Toll booth. Bicycles are free. A left takes you to the
  beach, picnic tables, restrooms, and a water spigot.

16.3 LEFT from the beach onto Moore Hill Rd. to continue the ride through the Forest. You will pass the road to the Campground and the Nature Center on your left and the trail to the Fire Tower on your right before coming to the back gate.

18.1 The back gate may be closed and you may have to dismount to get around it.

18.3 STRAIGHT onto Ludwig Rd. at the intersection with West Rd. and downhill.

19.1 RIGHT on Williamsburg Rd. and away you go, downhill all the way back to Williamsburg!

25.4 STRAIGHT onto Rte. 9 at the Williams House Restaurant. The Williamsburg General Store awaits you, just past the Historical Society and the Grange.

5

The Don Maynard Memorial Ride

Rating: Intermediate
Distance: 45 miles
Terrain: Hilly
Towns: Greenfield, Leyden; Guilford, VT, Vernon, VT, and Northfield, Bernardston, Gill

Points of Interest: Greenfield Community College, Covered Bridge, Weatherhead Hollow Pond, Whistlestop General Store, Vernon Fishway, Streeter's General Store, Marshall's Country Corner, Bernardston Books, Green River Park

Description: Formerly dubbed the Guilford Connection by popular cyclist, Don Maynard (the ride's originator), this ride has been renamed the Don Maynard Memorial Ride by the Franklin-Hampshire Freewheelers in memory of Don, who met an untimely death in his Greenfield home. Contrary to what might be expected, this is a happy ride because Don was a happy person and he would want it that way. If you feel the presence of a smiling bicyclist at your side saying, "How're you doing?" -- it's Don. This popular ride has become an annual event with the Freewheelers. Starting at Greenfield Community College, it immediately enters scenic countryside which continues into rural Vermont and back into Franklin County. Although it includes 1600 feet of climbing, the climbing is interspersed with long downhills, and much of it is flat. A leisurely pace and appropriately spaced rest stops make this a most enjoyable ride, and the scenery is tops.

Special care should be exercised while descending Eunice Williams Drive, a highly curving road that includes two horseshoe curves. A covered bridge with raised planks for automobile tires is at the foot of this hill. You are advised to dismount and walk through the bridge for safety reasons. This will also provide you with the opportunity to read the nearby markers which explain the historical significance of Eunice Williams.

On entering Vermont, there is a short stretch of hard-packed gravel followed by a lovely pond that provides a pleasant rest stop. The route passes through Guilford, Vermont, and the Whistle Stop General Store and Deli in Vernon provides a good place to stop for lunch. The Vernon Fishway makes another interesting stop if the shad are running. Numerous scenic spots en route invite a pause to rest and enjoy the views. Only a gravel pit along the way detracts from the scenery. Back in Massachusetts, either of two general stores in Bernardston provide the opportunity for another refreshment stop. The Bernardston Town Park or a grassy lawn and some shade trees on Barton Rd. invite additional rest stops. The remainder of the ride is pleasant, ending at Greenfield Community College.

Directions:
START from Greenfield Community College off Colrain Rd.
    in Greenfield.
0.0 EXIT the GCC parking lot onto College Drive.
0.6 LEFT onto Colrain Rd.
1.6 BEAR RIGHT onto Plain Rd. and into the countryside.
4.4 RIGHT onto Eunice Williams Drive. DANGER: Steep,
    winding downhill with horseshoe curves and a dark
    covered bridge with raised planks and sand at the
    bottom -- Ride slowly and carefully, or walk!
5.1 LEFT onto Greenfield road and uphill for 1.3 miles.
    Hang in there - a downhill will follow.

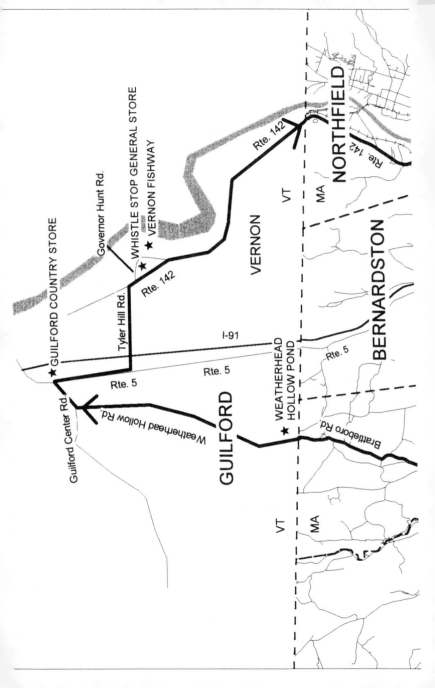

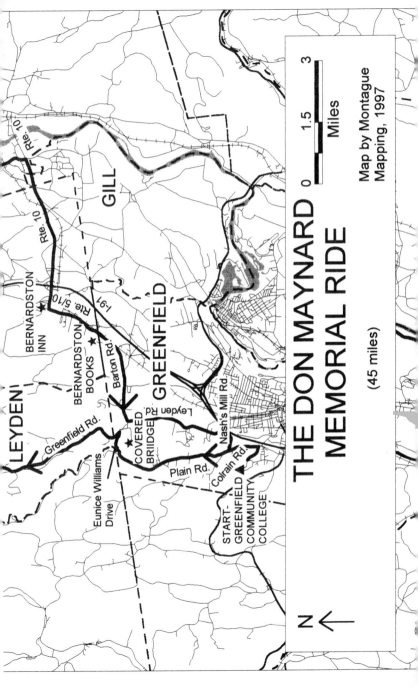

THE DON MAYNARD MEMORIAL RIDE

(45 miles)

Map by Montague
Mapping, 1997

8.8 BEAR RIGHT onto Brattleboro Rd. The Leyden Elementary School, hidden at first, will be on your right.

11.9 Vermont State Line. The road becomes hardpacked gravel and the road name changes to Weatherhead Hollow Road.

12.3 Weatherhead Hollow Pond is a scenic resting spot.

17.0 RIGHT onto Guilford Center Rd. along Broad Brook. It's mainly downhill.

18.7 RIGHT onto Rte. 5 South in Guilford. The Guilford Country Store across the road at the turn is closed on Sunday. Cross over Broad Brook.

21.0 LEFT onto Tyler Hill Rd. It's a short up, a long down, and very scenic.

23.3 RIGHT at the Stop Sign onto Rte. 142

23.6 Caution - railroad tracks! Cross at a diagonal. RIGHT to stay on Rte. 142.

23.8 LEFT into Whistle Stop General Store and Deli for food and a pit stop. There are tables inside and out, plus a front porch or a grassy lawn on which to sit.

23.9 RIGHT onto Governor Hunt Rd. behind the Whistle Stop.

24.7 LEFT into the Vernon Fishway (if it's open) for a view of fish climbing the ladder. Go down the steps to watch the fish through the windows. Go up another set of steps to access the restrooms.

24.8 STRAIGHT onto Rte. 142 South at the Stop Sign.

26.8 Schoolhouse Grocery. Stop if you need to refuel.

29.2 Welcome back to Massachusetts!

32.7 Caution! Railroad tracks again.

33.3 RIGHT onto Rte. 10 South. Watch for Streeter's General Store on your left or Marshall's Country Corner on your right.

36.4 LEFT onto Rte. 5 South at the Bernardston Inn (on your right) and the Town Park (on your left)

37.5 BEAR RIGHT onto Barton Rd. just beyond Bernardston Books, a second-hand book barn set back from the road.

40.5 LEFT onto Leyden Rd.

43.1 RIGHT onto Nash's Mill Rd., which comes up suddenly. If you cross over Rte. 91 you've gone too far. Pass Green River Park, or stop for a rest or swim.

43.7 LEFT onto Colrain Rd. The end is in sight.

44.5 RIGHT onto College Drive.

45.1 LEFT into the Greenfield Community College Parking Lot and the end of a glorious ride. Thank you, Don. Your ride and your memory live on.

6

Double Down

Rating: Novice
Distance: 21 miles
Terrain: Flat to rolling
Towns: Whately, Hatfield, Northampton, Leeds, Haydenville

Points of Interest: Whately town center, Hatfield Center's historic homes, Look Park

Description: This ride gets its name by starting and ending with a downhill. The route begins in Whately, a picturesque, upland meadow town with maple-lined streets. It's a sleepy town now, but it was once exceedingly busy with various mills and factories, an iron works, and gin distillery. Pottery was made from local clay. There is an excellent view of the Connecticut River Valley from behind the Town Hall, and the popular Whately Inn is located in the center of town. The route continues through scenic agricultural land to Hatfield, another attractive New England town with grand old houses lining the tree-shaded streets. Sophia Smith, founder of Smith College, was born here. Broom-making from locally grown corn was an early industry until tobacco took over in 1875.

From Hatfield the route leads to Look Park in Northampton. Here you can switch from pedaling on land to pedaling on water, take a miniature train ride, visit a small wildlife zoo, play a game of miniature golf, drive the bumper boats, picnic, or just bicycle through. Its a good place for a snack stop. The Visitors' Center has rest rooms and running water and can furnish you with information and a map of the park.

The route returns to Whately via Leeds and Haydenville, which are actually parts of Northampton. The downhill at the end is a nice way to end the ride. However, if you like hills, and some cyclists do, you might prefer to do this ride in reverse.

Directions:
START from the Whately Town Hall in the center of Whately.

0.0 LEFT onto Chestnut Plain Rd., which becomes Pantry Rd. in Hatfield.

3.3 RIGHT onto Rtes. 5 & 10 South.

6.7 RIGHT onto Hatfield St.

7.4 RIGHT onto Bridge Rd.

9.2 LEFT then RIGHT into Look Park. Bear right and bike the circuit through the park. Stop as you please. Enjoy!

10.5 STRAIGHT toward the Exit.

10.8 LEFT onto Rte. 9 West.

11.3 LEFT at the Y intersection onto Florence St.

11.5 LEFT onto Arch St. Caution: BLIND corner!

11.9 RIGHT onto Main St. in Leeds.

12.3 LEFT onto Mulberry St.

12.5 RIGHT onto River Rd.

13.8 RIGHT onto Bridge St. (No sign at this writing).

13.9 Cross Rte. 9 onto High St. which becomes Mountain St., then becomes Haydenville Rd.

19.0 LEFT to stay on Haydenville Rd.

20.6 LEFT onto Chestnut Plain at the T intersection and RIGHT at the Town Hall. Go out back to enjoy the view. This is a pleasant place to sit, relax and meditate on the beauty of our New England landscape.

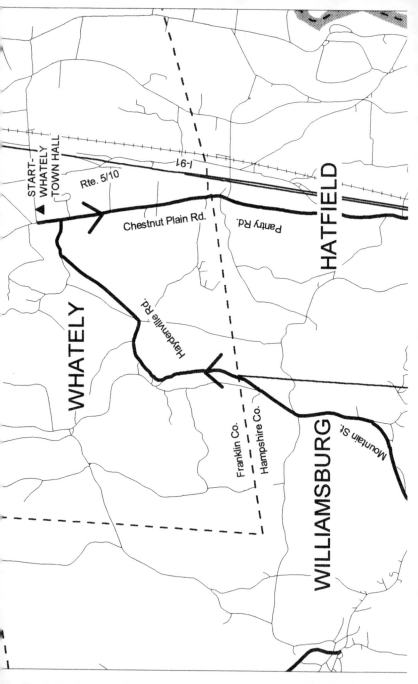

START- WHATELY TOWN HALL

Rte. 5/10

I-91

Chestnut Plain Rd.

Pantry Rd.

WHATELY

HATFIELD

Haydenville Rd.

Franklin Co.

Hampshire Co.

WILLIAMSBURG

Mountain St.

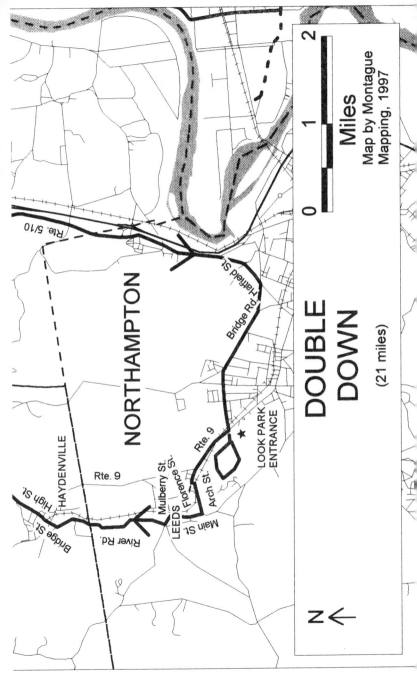

DOUBLE
DOWN

(21 miles)

NORTHAMPTON

Rte. 5/10

Bridge Rd

Hatfield St

Rte. 9

HAYDENVILLE

High St.

Bridge St.

River Rd.

Rte. 9

Mulberry St.

LEEDS

Florence St.

Arch St.

Main St.

LOOK PARK
ENTRANCE

Miles

Map by Montague
Mapping, 1997

0   1   2

N ←

7

Going to the Chapel

Rating: Novice to Intermediate
Distance: 14 to 25 miles
Terrain: Flat to hilly
Towns: Williamsburg, Conway, Ashfield, Whately

Points of Interest: Chapelbrook Reservation, Bakers Country Store, Northampton Reservoir, Nash Hill School, Williamsburg General Store

Description: This is a very pretty ride on lightly traveled roads. Although the hills might be challenging to the novice rider, an energetic novice in good condition can ride at least as far as Chapelbrook Reservation and possibly the entire ride. It's a fairly gradual uphill made easier with occasional stopping to enjoy the scenery or walk. Reversing direction at Chapelbrook Reservation shortens the ride to 14 miles, and it's downhill on the way back.

The route takes you through an attractive residential area which soon gives way to woods, fields, and streams. Chapel Falls and Chapel Ledge are the real highlights of the ride, but the entire route is scenic and there's a great downhill from South Ashfield to Conway. From there the route cuts over to Whately and back to Williamsburg, a section which includes woods and farmland and passes by Northampton Reservoir. The home stretch includes about two miles of hard-packed gravel and one short hill, but ends in a beautiful downhill.

Directions:

START from the parking area behind the Williamsburg
   Historical Society and the Historic Williams House
   Restaurant on Rte. 9 in Williamsburg. Enter the parking
   area by the driveway between the Grange and the
   Historical Society.

0.0 LEFT on Rte. 9 from the above driveway.

0.1 BEAR RIGHT on North St., cross North Main St. and
   remain on North St., which begins as an attractive
   residential area and almost immediately becomes a very
   pretty wooded country road with a stream on the right.

0.5 North St. becomes Ashfield Rd.

3.2 BEAR LEFT on Ashfield Rd. where it intersects with
   Conway Rd.

4.2 Conway Town Line. Ashfield Rd. becomes Williamsburg
   Rd. and the uphill becomes more serious.

5.3 At Main Poland Rd., stop and look back at the beautiful
   view which includes Mt. Tom, then continue on up South
   Ashfield Rd.

5.8 Ashfield Town Line.

6.4 PASS Ludwig Rd. on your left, which cuts over to D.A.R.
   State Forest. (See *D.A.R. State Forest*, Ride 4)

7.0 Chapelbrook Reservation: Just off the road on your
   right, which may or may not have a sign, is a short
   path on the left which leads down to Chapel Falls, a
   cascade over three ledges. Take a break, take a walk,
   and enjoy! Across the road on your left, a path leads
   up to Chapel Ledge, a sheer 80-foot granite cliff which is
   popular with rock climbers. Follow the yellow-blazed
   trail on the left and go to the top for a spectacular view.
   It's an easy hike and a great lunch stop. Back on the
   road again, at the top of the hill, you will pass a
   typical New England farm with an old farmhouse on the
   left and a big barn and an apple orchard on the right.

9.3 RIGHT on Rte. 116 for a long downhill into Conway.

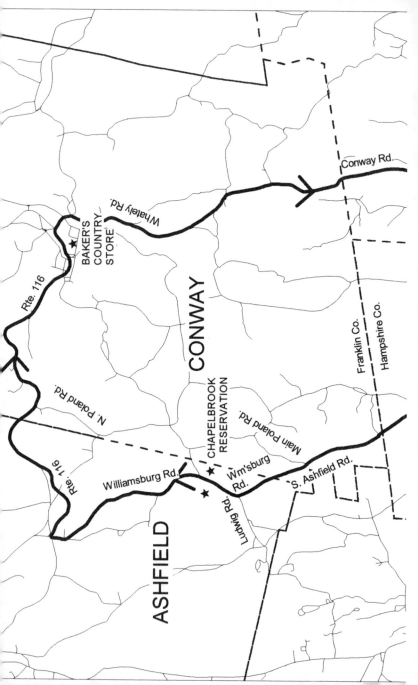

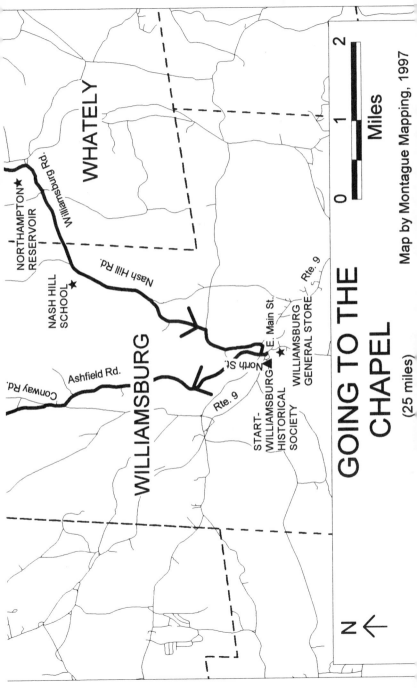

GOING TO THE CHAPEL

(25 miles)

Map by Montague Mapping, 1997

11.5 PASS North Poland Rd. on your right.

14.4 STOP at Baker's Country Store and Luncheonette on your right for coffee and homemade baked goods. Their apple fritters are great! There's a restroom in the rear of the store on the left.

14.9 RIGHT on Whately Rd. between the playing field (site of Festival of the Hills) and the grassy triangle, then past the United Congregational Church.

15.2 LEFT at the Y intersection uphill. Don't worry; a long flat stretch follows. Whately Rd. will become Conway Rd. in Whately.

19.7 PASS the Northampton Reservoir on your right.

20.1 RIGHT on Williamsburg Rd. and over a bridge at the end of the Reservoir. The road will turn to hard-packed gravel for about two miles, with a short hill just before it becomes pavement again. Hang in there. The long, scenic downhill that follows is worth it.

22.4 The Nash Hill School, a little red schoolhouse (1718-1917), is set back from the road on your right. Pause, then prepare for a long, paved downhill past historic homes into Williamsburg on Nash Hill Rd.

24.5 BEAR RIGHT at the intersection onto East Main St., then left onto North Main St. and Rte. 9.

24.6 RIGHT on Williams Rd. at the Williams House Restaurant and left into the parking lot from which you started the ride, or stay on Rte. 9 and continue a short distance to the Williamsburg General Store for ice cream and coffee before returning to the parking lot.

8

Look Park
via the Northampton Bike Path
and Norwottuck Rail Trail

Rating: Novice
Distance: 7 to 16 miles
Terrain: Flat
Towns: Hadley, Northampton

Points of Interest: Pedal boats, picnic area and store, train ride, petting zoo, miniature golf, and bumper boats at Look Park; Bread & Circus Natural Food Store, Pete's Drive-in, tunnel under Rte. 9, old railroad bridge over the Connecticut River on the Norwottuck Rail Trail.

Description: The shorter version of this ride is appropriate for families with small children who aren't ready to ride on roads but can manage the Northampton Bike Path. The longer ride uses this path as well as the Norwottuck Rail Trail and includes a stretch of busy road where it is absolutely essential to keep to the right and ride single file. To learn more about the Northampton Bike Path and the Norwottuck Rail Trail, refer to *Great Rail-Trails of the Northeast* (see References, page 167).

Both the short and long rides go to Look Park, a lovely spot and fun for young and old. If you're tired of pedaling your bicycle try pedaling a boat; it's a new experience. The miniature train ride and the zoo are fun, too. Miniature golf and bumper boats are the latest attractions. Picnic tables must be reserved but there are benches and plenty of grass. Admission is free to bicyclists. Stop at the Visitors' Center for further information and a map or to use the restrooms.

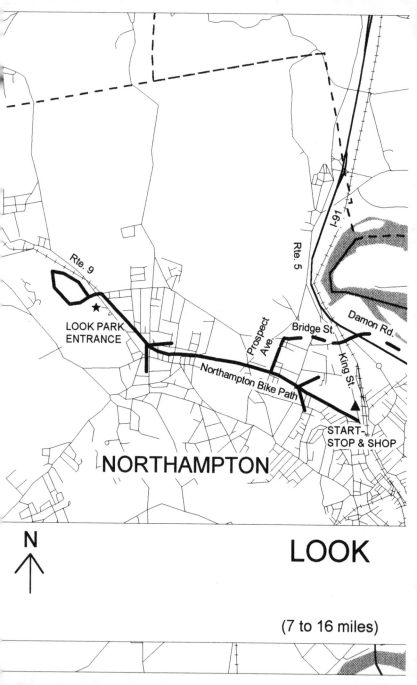

Rte. 9

LOOK PARK
ENTRANCE

Rte. 5

I-91

Damon Rd.

Prospect Ave.

Bridge St.

King St.

Northampton Bike Path

START-
STOP & SHOP

NORTHAMPTON

N

LOOK

(7 to 16 miles)

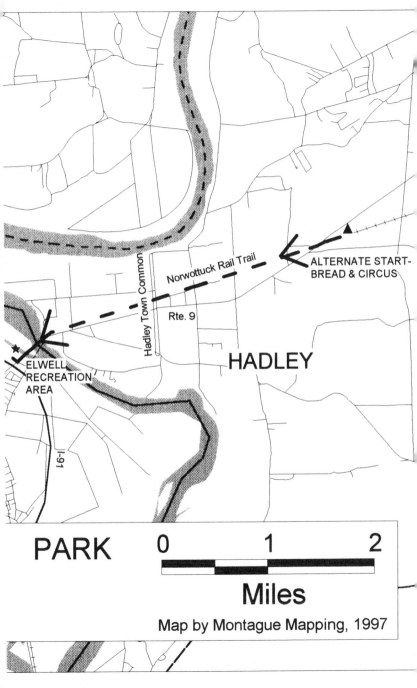

ALTERNATE START-
BREAD & CIRCUS

Norwottuck Rail Trail

Hadley Town Common

Rte. 9

HADLEY

ELWELL
RECREATION
AREA

I-91

PARK

0   1   2

Miles

Map by Montague Mapping, 1997

Directions for the shorter ride:

START from the parking lot between the Stop and Shop supermarket and Liquors 44 on Rtes. 5 & 10, located north of Rte. 9 and south of Damon and Bridge Roads in Northampton. There is a paved access to the Bike Path behind the Stop and Shop. Look for the yellow poles.

0.0 RIGHT onto the bike path. Watch for pedestrians and skaters. Keep to the right. Dismount at street crossings and look both ways before crossing.

2.7 LEFT and use the sidewalk to the cross walk to the Look Park entrance. Cross Rte. 9. Caution: this is a busy traffic section.

2.8 STRAIGHT to enter the park. Bikes enter free!

2.9 RIGHT to follow the one-way loop around the park. You may use the road or the bike/pedestrian path that winds through the park. The milepoints are for road travel.

3.0 Visitors Center: Information, maps, and restrooms are available. Miniature golf course and bumper boat rides are also here.

3.4 The pedal boat pond is on the left. Restrooms are on the right.

3.5 Small play area.

3.9 Picnic store.

4.0 Big play area.

4.1 LEFT to go to the train station and the petting zoo. This will add a small amount of mileage.

4.15 STRAIGHT to exit.

4.3 EXIT through gates to Rte. 9.

4.35 LEFT on Rte. 9, then right to get to the sidewalk.

4.4 RIGHT onto the bike path

7.0 Yellow poles and parking lot. End of the ride.

Directions for the longer ride:

START from behind and to the right of the Bread and Circus
    Natural Foods Store parking lot, off Rte. 9 in Hadley.
    Food and restrooms available in Bread and Circus.
0.0 RIGHT onto the Norwottuck Rail Trail. Keep to the
    right and watch for pedestrians and skateboarders as
    well as other bicyclists.
0.3 Pete's Drive In: Telephone, food, bike tools, and restroom
    available. Pete's caters especially to cyclists.
0.4 SOUND horn or bell, or yell, before entering the tunnel
    under Rte. 9.
2.0 OBSERVE Stop signs before crossing the Hadley
    Common. Watch for the Valley Bicycles Trailside
    on your left.
3.0 OBSERVE the Stop sign and look carefully before
    crossing the road just before the old railroad bridge --
    there is a blind crossing on the right.
3.3 CROSS over the bridge carefully. People tend to stop
    on the bridge. Ring, honk or holler before passing.
3.7 You have arrived in the Elwell Recreation Area of
    Connecticut River Greenway State Park. There is a
    composting toilet to your left but no running water.
    Across the road there's the Fish Hook Restaurant and a
    Bananarama soft ice cream and frozen yogurt stand.
3.8 RIGHT on Damon Rd. This is a busy stretch of road with
    almost no shoulder. Ride single file and keep to the
    right.
4.7 CAUTION: Look, signal, and move to the middle lane
    to cross over Rtes. 5 & 10 and onto Bridge Rd.
4.9 STRAIGHT at the light to remain on Bridge Rd.
5.2 LEFT on Prospect Ave.

5.5 RIGHT at the green gate onto Northampton's Bike Path.

7.3 LEFT onto the sidewalk. Ride to the cross-walk to cross Rte. 9. Watch for traffic!

7.4 ENTER Look Park. Autos pay; bikes are free!

7.5 RIGHT and follow the one-way loop around the park.

7.6 Visitors Center: Information, map, restroom. Miniature golf and bumper boats are also here.

8.0 Pedal boat pond on the left. Restrooms on the right.

8.1 Small play area

8.4 Optional left to go to the pedal boats.

8.5 Picnic Store.

8.6 Big play area.

8.7 Optional left to go to the train station and the petting zoo.

8.7 STRAIGHT to go to the exit.

8.9 Exit through the gates back to Rte. 9.

8.95 LEFT onto Rte. 9, then right onto the sidewalk.

9.0 RIGHT onto the Northampton Bike Path.

10.8 LEFT on Prospect Ave.

11.1 RIGHT onto Bridge Rd.

11.4 STRAIGHT at the light to remain on Bridge Rd.

11.6 STRAIGHT at the light across Rtes. 5 & 10 onto Damon Rd. Traffic can be heavy.

12.5 LEFT into Elwell State Recreation Area at the light and onto the Norwottuck Rail Trail, then back to Bread and Circus. Observe all previous warnings.

16.2 LEFT into the Bread and Circus parking lot Refreshments and restrooms are available in Bread and Circus where cyclists are welcome.

9

Mountain Laurel and Lakes

Rating: Intermediate
Distance: 36 miles
Terrain: Moderately hilly
Towns: Brimfield and Holland, Massachusetts; Union and Stafford, Connecticut; Wales, Massachusetts

Points of Interest: Brimfield Common, Mill Pond, Windmill House, Lake Siog, Hamilton Reservoir, Laurel Sanctuary, Staffordville Reservoir, Lake George

Description: This ride is best enjoyed in June when the mountain laurel is in bloom. It is a scenic ride at anytime of year, but in June it's spectacular! Plan to have a picnic lunch at Laurel Reservation in Nipmuck State Forest in Union, Connecticut. In a small clearing with a beautiful old maple tree there is a picnic table tucked away in the back corner among the laurel bushes. If that is already in use, there is a bench in a clearing further along the road, and beyond that there is another clearing where you can sit on the grass. This ride follows country roads past woods, fields, farms, ponds, and lakes. Swim stops are possible and there are several opportunities for food stops along the first section of the ride. Although the terrain is hilly, the hills are gradual, and if you pace yourself they aren't bad. Hills have their own rewards and this ride has great downhills.

Brimfield, where the ride begins and ends, becomes a giant antique market during one week in May, July, and September. You may want to avoid those periods unless you're into antiques. The highway becomes very congested with cars and antiquers.

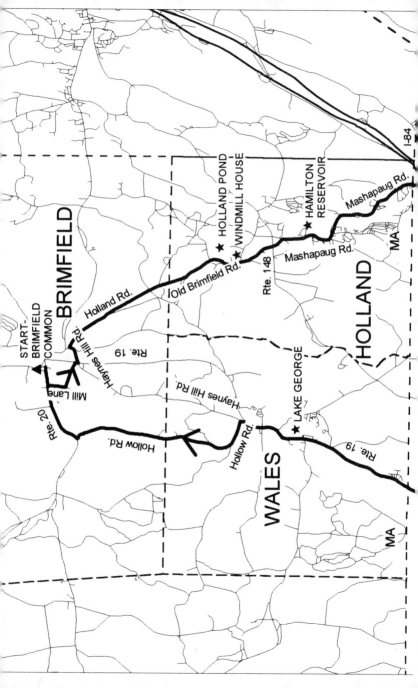

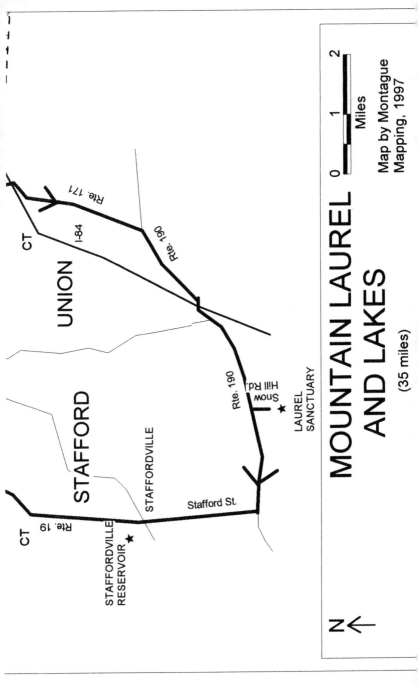

MOUNTAIN LAUREL AND LAKES

(35 miles)

Map by Montague Mapping, 1997

You can lengthen this ride by continuing on Rte. 190 to Stafford Springs, Connecticut, then taking Rte. 32 north to Brimfield Road to Monson, Massachusetts, and east to Brimfield. You can also shorten it by beginning and ending the ride in Wales and then use North Wales Road as a connecting road with the town of Holland.

Directions:

START at the Brimfield Common on Rte. 20. Park on the right opposite the shops at the end of the Common.

0.0 STRAIGHT or west on Rte. 20 and past the white frame church and Town Hall on your right.

0.3 LEFT onto Mill Lane Rd. and into the country.

0.5 CROSS the old trolley road to Worcester, then pass a lovely Mill Pond on your right. The mill is no longer present; only the pond remains. Enjoy the lovely view.

1.0 Pass Brimfield Precision, Inc., manufacturer of artificial limbs.

1.1 RIGHT onto Rte. 19, then an immediate right onto Haynes Hill Rd.

1.5 RIGHT onto Holland Rd., parallel to the trolley tracks, then straight onto Brimfield Rd. (Bear right then left).

5.2 Pass a road on the left that leads to Lake Siog Park or Holland Pond, which has swimming and picnicking.

5.8 A windmill house is on your left and, yes, you're in Holland. Across the street is Holland Pizza. Old Brimfield Rd. will become Mashapaug Rd. at Hamilton Reservoir.

6.5 Lake Massaconnet or Hamilton Reservoir is on your left and Holland Market on your right. As for the name of the lake, the first name connects Mass. with Conn., as does the lake. The second name is based on the fact that Hamilton Woolen used the lake for power. There is a small cluster of eating places in the vicinity and a Sani-Can on the beach.

7.0 BEAR LEFT on Mashapaug Rd. and cross over the lake, which will then be on your right.

8.9 Connecticut State Line at the town of Union. The lake continues and there is a convenience store and restaurant on your right.

9.4 LEFT and cross over I-84.

9.5 RIGHT on 171 East, which parallels I-84.

11.4 Observe the Charcoal Kilns on your left.

11.9 STRAIGHT onto Rte. 190. Pass the road to Bigelow State Park on your left.

12.2 BEAR RIGHT and continue on Rte. 190 at a Y-intersection, small triangular park with a cannon, monument and small building. Historians may want to stop here.

14.0 CROSS I-84 again.

15.3 LEFT on Snow Hill Rd. (hard-packed gravel) and into Laurel Sanctuary of Nipmuck State Forest. Look for the picnic table on your right, the bench on your left or the grassy plot for lunch. Enjoy the laurel display.

16.2 The laurel ends here. Turn around and return to 190.

17.0 LEFT on 190 for a long, well-deserved downhill past more laurel bushes, primarily on your left, and a lily pond. The terrain becomes rolling but downhills continue.

18.7 Stafford Town Line.

21.9 RIGHT on Stafford St., uphill then rolling. Pass Stafford Springs Town Line at a Common on your left.

22.0 BEAR RIGHT and downhill.

23.7 BEAR RIGHT again and downhill to stay on Stafford St.

24.8 RIGHT into Staffordville and onto Rte. 19. Pass the Staffordville Reservoir on your left.

28.0 Massachusetts State Line at the town of Wales.

30.0 Pass Lake George on your right.

30.3 The benches and tiny beach on your right invite a rest.

30.6 The white pillared Town Hall is on your left.

31.2 BEAR LEFT on Haynes Hill Rd., then an IMMEDIATE LEFT on Hollow Rd. for a long downhill to Rte. 20.

34.5 RIGHT on Rte. 20

35.9 Brimfield Common. End of ride.

10

Mount Tom
and the Dinosaur Tracks

Rating: Novice to Intermediate
Distance: 15 miles
Terrain: Flat to hilly
Towns: Easthampton, Holyoke

Points of Interest: Oxbow, Mount Tom State Reservation, Dinosaur Tracks along the Connecticut River

Description: This short, interesting ride has one significant uphill within Mt Tom State Reservation but is otherwise relatively easy, and the downhill exceeds the uphill in mileage. The 1800-acre forested Reservation lies within the cities of Holyoke and Easthampton, and features an extensive hiking trail system as well as the Metacomet-Monadnock Trail which traverses the entire State. Picnic tables and vistas are interspersed throughout the park and an observation tower on Goat Peak is popular with birdwatchers during the annual hawk migration in the fall. Bray Lake provides recreational activities including picnicking, fishing and skating.

The roads used to and from the Reservation include a scenic stretch of Route 5 with wide paved shoulders and a long downhill on Route 141. Only a very short stretch travels through a business area, and that is followed by an attractive residential area. After passing the entrance to the Mount Tom Ski Area (a water theme park in summer), the route goes downhill to the Dinosaur Footprints Reservation along the Connecticut River. The red sandstone footprint area is considered one of the finest Triassic beds in the world.

Back on Route 5 again, the route follows the river back to the Oxbow and the ride's end. The Oxbow is a body of water created when the river relocated itself during a 19th century flood. It is now a recreational area, popular with boaters in the summer and ice fishers in the winter. It still connects to the river, and a small stream adjacent to Massachusetts Audubon's Arcadia Wildlife Sanctuary provides access to it.

Directions:
START from the parking area at the Oxbow State Ramp for
    Boats, located on Rte. 5 in Easthampton beside the
    Electric Midway Substation.
0.0 RIGHT (South) on Rte. 5 towards Holyoke.
0.1 CROSS the railroad tracks, pass Oxbow Sports and
    continue on Rte. 5 on the wide paved shoulder.
0.7 PASS the Mount Tom Power Station on your left.
1.1 PASS the entrance to the Holyoke Country Club.
1.4 PASS the Delaney House Restaurant.
1.9 RIGHT at the entrance to Mount Tom State Reservation
    opposite the Competitive Edge Ski and Bicycle store and
    through a residential area to the inner gate.
2.2 STRAIGHT past gate and under Interstate 91. It's a
    short uphill followed by a downhill to Bray Lake.
2.4 PASS Bray Lake or take a short break there. There are
    picnic tables and portable toilets. Hiking trails start from
    both sides of the lake. Prepare for 1.5 miles of steep uphill
    with short intervals of relative flatness; a rewarding
    downhill follows.
3.9 LEFT at the intersection. If you have time, a right turn
    will take you on a side trip to Mount Nonotuck, Goat
    Peak, and the Lookout Tower (popular with birders in
    the fall during the hawk migration). Otherwise, our route
    goes left and you'll like it; it's scenic and flat. You will
    pass some picnic tables and three vistas as well as some
    impressive boulders before beginning a welcome
    downhill.

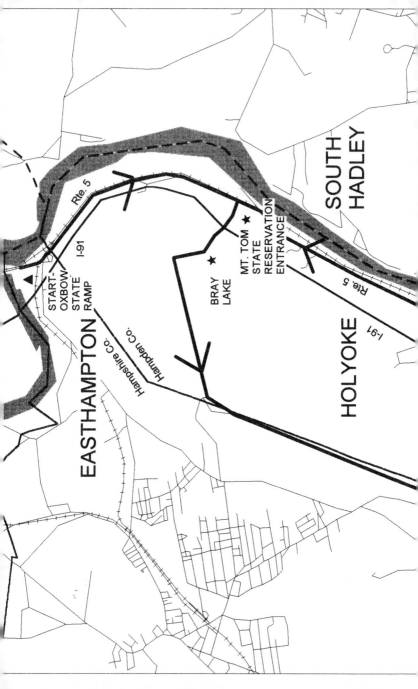

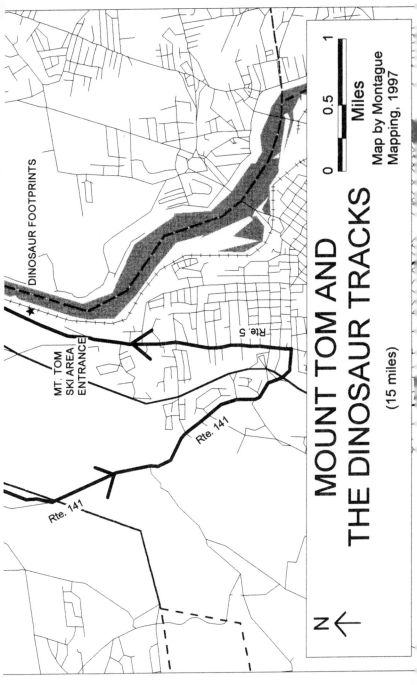

MOUNT TOM AND
THE DINOSAUR TRACKS

(15 miles)

N

DINOSAUR FOOTPRINTS

MT. TOM SKI AREA ENTRANCE

Rte. 5

Rte. 141

Rte. 141

Miles

0   0.5   1

Map by Montague
Mapping, 1997

6.2 LEFT on Rte. 141 opposite the Harvest Valley Restaurant and more downhill (all the way to Rte. 5).

7.3 PASS Wyckoff Country Club on your left. Rte. 141 will become one way up ahead.

8.6 LEFT on Rte. 5 at the lights after getting into the left lane.

8.8 STRAIGHT through the second set of lights, into a residential section known as the Highlands. There are many lovely homes in this part of town.

10.2 PASS the road which leads up to the Mount Tom Ski Area on your left. A downhill stretch will lead you to a pullover on your right. Pull over.

10.8 STOP: Its the Dinosaur Footprints Reservation. Lock your bike to the railing or wheel it down the path that leads to the footprints and lock it to a tree. The path divides and the boardwalk to the left leads you to the footprints. The path to the right leads you down to the Connecticut River. Visit that, too. Then return to Rte. 5 and continue northward. The river will be on your right.

12.6 PASS the entrance to Mount Tom State Reservation on your left, which you turned up at the beginning of the ride.

14.5 CROSS the railroad tracks again.

14.6 LEFT into the Oxbow parking area. End of ride.

11

Northfield Ramble

Rating: Novice to Intermediate
Distance: 20 or 29 miles
Terrain: Flat to moderately hilly
Towns: Greenfield, Turners Falls, Northfield, Gill

Points of Interest: Discovery Center, Fish Ladder, Millers River Bridge, Riverview Picnic Area, Northfield Mountain Recreation and Environmental Center, The Gill Store, Turners Falls Village

Description: This scenic ride includes a portion of the proposed Franklin County Bikeway. From Greenfield it continues through the historic mill village of Turners Falls and wends its way along the beautiful Connecticut River, through woods and farmland, across the Millers River bridge (for pedestrians and bicyclists only), then under the French King Bridge spanning the Connecticut River. It stops at a beautiful picnic area along the river, and there is an option to visit the Northfield Mountain Recreation and Environmental Center. Proceeding up river and then out to Route 63, the ride heads west and south through Gill to Turners Falls, where it crosses the canal and river and then returns to Greenfield. Although this route starts at the Franklin County Courthouse in Greenfield, it can also start and end at the Discovery Center in Turners Falls and be a 19.6 mile ride. Other options for shortening the route appear in the directions.

Directions:
START at the parking area of the Franklin County
    Courthouse in Greenfield

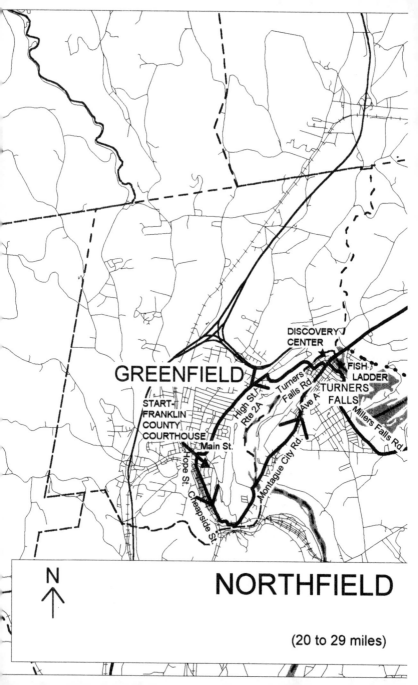

DISCOVERY
CENTER

FISH
LADDER

GREENFIELD

Turners
Falls Rd.

TURNERS
FALLS

START-
FRANKLIN
COUNTY
COURTHOUSE

High St.
Rte 2A

Ave A

Millers Falls Rd.

Main St.

Montague City Rd.

Hope St.

Cheapside St.

N

NORTHFIELD

(20 to 29 miles)

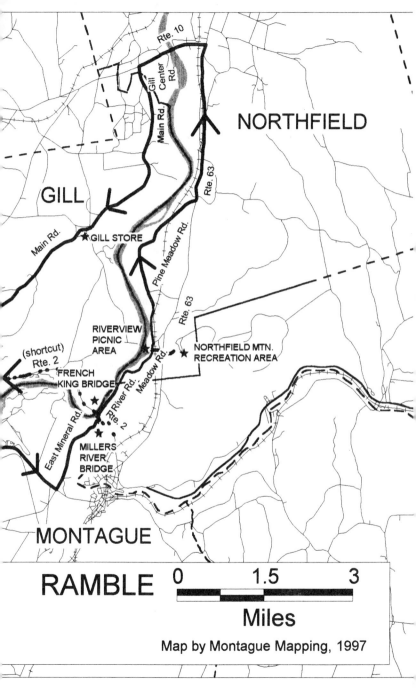

NORTHFIELD

GILL

Rte. 10

Gill Center Rd.

Main Rd.

Rte. 63

Main Rd.

★ GILL STORE

Pine Meadow Rd.

Rte. 63

RIVERVIEW PICNIC AREA

NORTHFIELD MTN. RECREATION AREA

(shortcut) Rte. 2

FRENCH KING BRIDGE

East Mineral Rd.

River Rd.

Meadow Rd.

Rte. 2

MILLERS RIVER BRIDGE

MONTAGUE

RAMBLE

0   1.5   3

Miles

Map by Montague Mapping, 1997

0.0 LEFT onto Hope St. and downhill. CAUTION! Curves, underpass, and left turn at the bottom of the hill.

1.3 LEFT onto Cheapside St., which will become Montague City Rd.

2.2 CROSS the bridge over the Connecticut River into Turners Falls. CAUTION! The bridge is bumpy. Restrooms and refreshments are available at the Cumberland Farms and Gulf Station on your left en route.

4.6 STOP at the Discovery Center. Look at the mural on the outside wall and the maps in the windows. If the Center is open, look at the displays, pick up informational pamphlets, and use the restroom if necessary.

4.6 RIGHT on First Avenue, just past the Shady Glen Restaurant

4.7 PASS the sign for the Fish Ladder and Picnic Area along the Connecticut River on your left. The Fish Ladder is generally open for viewing Wed. through Sun. from mid-May through mid-June or the end of the run. Time it right and you may see the shad run -- maybe a salmon. There are restrooms here and a viewing telescope (usually focused on an eagle's nest in Barton Cove).

4.9 Barton Cove is off to your left. A short uphill begins here. For a shorter, flatter ride reverse direction and return to the Discovery Center. (See milepoint 25.6 for a different route back.)

5.1 LEFT onto Unity St. to continue the ride.

5.4 BEAR LEFT onto High St.

5.5 BEAR LEFT onto Millers Falls Rd., which begins a long, flat stretch of easy riding.

8.3 LEFT on East Mineral Rd. Pass an old cemetery on your left and continue through a wooded area.

9.0 Open fields and farmland begin a long downhill. EXTREME CAUTION! Curves! Barrier at the bottom! (This barrier will be removed when the bridge is officially converted to a bicycle-pedestrian bridge.)

9.7 BARRIER! Lift your bike over the barrier onto the Millers River Bridge. Enjoy the view and notice the French King Bridge on your left. You'll be bicycling under it soon.

9.75 LEFT on River Road to Pine Meadow Rd.; go under the French King Bridge and alongside the Connecticut River.

10.4 CAUTION! Road changes to gravel for a stretch.

11.4 LEFT into the Riverview Picnic Area to have lunch, use the restrooms, or simply enjoy the beautiful view of the river before continuing on Pine Meadow Rd.

OPTION: A right from the picnic area will take you out to Route 63. Another right and a left will bring you to the Northfield Mt. Recreation and Environmental Center. Snacks, restrooms and exhibits (upper level) are inside.

OPTION TO SHORTEN RIDE: Reverse direction on Pine Meadow Rd., which becomes River Rd. and leads out to Rte. 2. Take Rte. 2 west and past the Barton Cove Campground to milepost 25.1 and cross the river into Turners Falls. Follow the return route from there.

11.6 LEFT onto Pine Meadow Rd. from Riverview Picnic Area to continue the 29-mile ride. The pavement will turn to gravel, then back to pavement. The road continues along the river and through farmland, including a turf farm. It's a very pretty stretch of road.

14.7 LEFT onto Rte. 63 just after a horse farm. You will pass a couple of historic markers along the way. Stop and read them for the history of the region.

17.3 LEFT on Rte. 10 South and cross the Connecticut River.

18.5 LEFT on Gill Center Rd. to Main Road Gill, a scenic stretch of farmland with many ups and downs (more down than up).

21.9 STOP at the historic Gill Store on your left (in continuous operation since 1803). It is closed Sundays.

23.9 CAUTION! A long downhill with traffic lights at the bottom.

25.1 Traffic lights! Cross Rte. 2 and the bridge over the Connecticut River into Turners Falls., an historic mill town.

25.6 RIGHT at the Discovery Center and onto Canal St.

25.9 RIGHT over the canal, then over the river into Greenfield and uphill on Turners Falls Rd., which will eventually become one way. At this point bear right onto Loomis.

26.9 LEFT at the T intersection onto Rte. 2A or High St. Pass the Franklin Medical Center.

28.6 RIGHT onto Main St.

28.7 LEFT onto Hope St.

28.8 LEFT into the Courthouse Parking Lot and end of ride.

12

Out of the Valley
and Up to Vermont

Rating: Intermediate
Distance: 36 miles
Terrain: Flat to hilly
Towns: Colrain, Massachusetts; Halifax, Jacksonville and
Whitingham, Vermont

Points of Interest: Halifax Gorge, North River Winery,
Jacksonville General Store, Harriman Reservoir

Description: The goal of this ride is a picnic and swim at
Harriman Reservoir, so pick a nice day. If the weather doesn't
cooperate, there are alternative activities and it's still a nice
ride, scenic from the very beginning. The route begins in
Colrain at the site of the first school to fly the United States
flag. A four-mile-long gradual uphill starts at the Jacksonville
General Store, which could be the endpoint of a shorter
version of this ride. Harriman Reservoir is reached by a
gravel road that requires some careful cycling, but it's a
beautiful spot to picnic, swim and relax. There are outhouses
and dressing rooms at the main area, but no running water. It
is recommended that you stop at Halifax Gorge and the North
River Winery on the way back.

Directions:
START from the Colrain Central Elementary School on Rte.
    112 in Colrain.
0.0 LEFT from the parking area onto Rte. 112 and you're in
    farming country -- and it's beautiful.

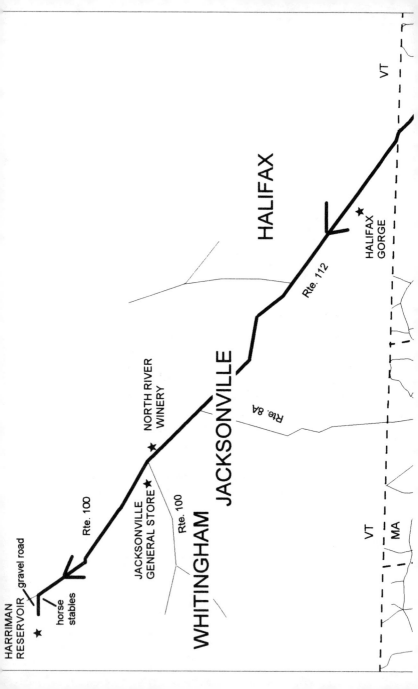

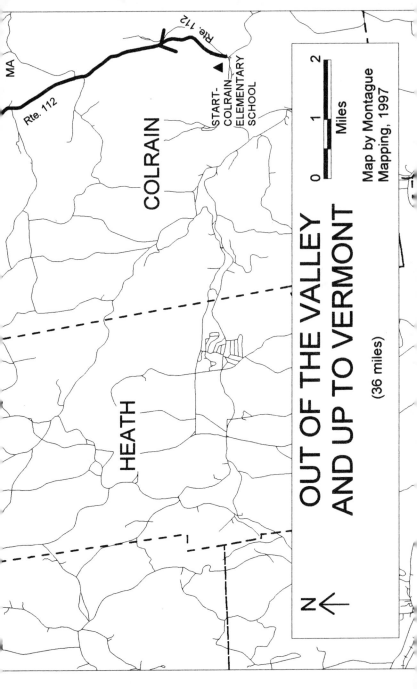

OUT OF THE VALLEY
AND UP TO VERMONT

(36 miles)

MA

Rte. 112

Rte. 112

START-
COLRAIN
ELEMENTARY
SCHOOL

COLRAIN

HEATH

N

Miles

0   1   2

Map by Montague
Mapping, 1997

4.0 CROSS the metal bridge over the North River with care. The North River accompanies you for most of the ride. Following snow melt in late winter/early spring, the river becomes a whitewater canoeing and kayaking stream.

4.7 Enter Vermont.

6.1 Halifax Gorge is on your left out of sight but can be reached by a steep path from one of two pullovers. The brave and foolish jump off the cliffs into a deep pool.

12.0 North River Winery on your right offers wine tastings and tours. Their wines include apple, raspberry, rhubarb and more.

12.1 RIGHT on Rte. 100 and stop at the Jacksonville General Store for coffee or a cold drink on the porch. You can also purchase the makings of a picnic lunch here.

12.2 LEFT to stay on Rte. 100. The uphill begins here.

12.7 There's spring water on your left.

16.4 HARD LEFT onto the gravel road that leads to Harriman Reservoir. There is a small cluster of mailboxes and a sign that says *Flames Stables*. The stables will be on your left. Continue STRAIGHT; no turns. The hard-packed gravel will become rougher as you approach the reservoir.

17.7 You've arrived. There are picnic areas on the hillside on the left and on the right both below and beyond the parking area. If you enjoy nude bathing, there is a path that leads to a wonderful rocky area to the far right. To exit the reservoir, return to Rte. 100 via the gravel road.

19.0 RIGHT onto Rte. 100 and a wonderful downhill.

23.2 RIGHT at the Jacksonville General Store. There's an antique store across the street.

23.3 LEFT onto Rte. 112

23.4 North River Winery. It's worth stopping here.

29.3 Halifax Gorge. Another swim, maybe?

30.7 Re-enter Massachusetts and the Pioneer Valley.

31.4 Cross over the bridge again.

35.4 RIGHT into the Colrain Central School parking lot.

13

Over to Otis

Rating: Intermediate to advanced
Distance: 55 miles (or less)
Terrain: Flat to hilly
Towns: Huntington, Chester, Blandford, Otis, Becket

Points of Interest: Westfield River, Huntington Country Store

Description: Although this ride strays into the Berkshires, it begins and ends in the Pioneer Valley, traversing three counties -- Hampshire, Hampden and Berkshire. The route is primarily flat at the beginning as it follows the Westfield River to Chester where it veers away from the river and uphill to Blandford. Here it flattens out and is followed by a long downhill, which more than compensates for the previous short steep uphill.

This is a lovely, scenic ride. Except for the first uphill, it is not difficult but should be avoided on a hot, humid day. This is a ride to be enjoyed at your own pace, resting as often as you like. It is advisable to carry snacks and a full water bottle, although there are places to buy food and drink en route. At the end of the ride you can rest and refuel on the porch of the Huntington Country Store with an ice cream, coffee, or cold drink.

It's possible to shorten this ride by starting somewhere along Route 20, but you would miss a lovely stretch on Basket Street and Old State Road along the Westfield River. Route 20 is a good bicycling route, so you might want to just do a stretch along Rte. 20 and skip the hills. Whatever you decide, it will be scenic.

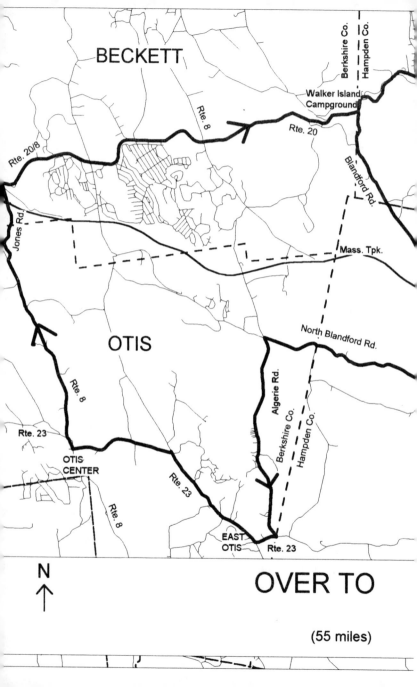

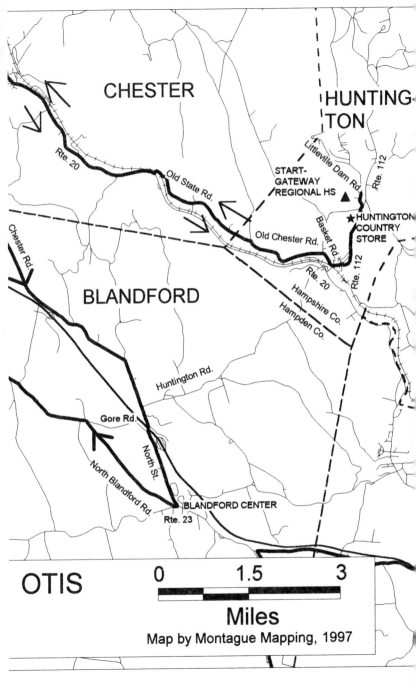

CHESTER

HUNTING-
TON

Rte. 20

Old State Rd.

Littleville Dam Rd.

Rte. 112

START-
GATEWAY
REGIONAL HS

Old Chester Rd.

Basket Rd.

HUNTINGTON
COUNTRY
STORE

Chester Rd.

BLANDFORD

Rte. 20

Rte. 112

Hampshire Co.

Hampden Co.

Huntington Rd.

Gore Rd.

North St.

North Blandford Rd.

BLANDFORD CENTER

Rte. 23

OTIS

0   1.5   3

Miles

Map by Montague Mapping, 1997

Directions:

START from the Gateway Regional High School parking lot
   on Littleville Dam Rd. off Rte. 112 in Huntington.

0.0 RIGHT on Littleville Dam Rd.

0.3 RIGHT on Rte. 112.

1.5 RIGHT on Basket St. at the sign "Middlefield 10" before
   the bridge over the Westfield River. Bear left to stay
   along the river at each intersection to the end of this
   road, which becomes Old State Rd. Cross the river.

5.5 RIGHT on Rte. 20 to Chester.

8.6 Mobil Station and Restaurant offers rest rooms and body
   fuel. Snacks are also available at Mary's Variety located
   at 0.25 mile further along the route.

10.2 LEFT just after Walker Island Campground and before
   the Becket Town Line, cross a bridge, go UP Blandford
   Road which becomes Chester Road in Blandford.

18.2 Pass the Blandford Country Club and a white church.

18.3 Right on Rte. 23, then an immediate right on North
   Blandford Rd. (no sign as of this writing)

24.9 Left at the Stop Sign onto Algerie Rd. (no sign).

28.4 RIGHT on Rte. 23 W.

28.8 There are a couple of general stores in East Otis: Katie's
   and Hall's. Hall's has an outhouse. Both have food.

32.5 RIGHT on Rte. 8 in Otis.

35.9 RIGHT just after the Farm Store, up Jones to Becket Rd.

37.3 RIGHT on Rte. 20 E.

40.1 Ice cream and rest rooms at Bob and Rita's, then enjoy
   the long downhill almost all the way into Huntington.

49.1 LEFT onto Old State Rd., over the bridge and along
   the river.

53.1 LEFT onto Rte. 112.

54.2 LEFT at the Huntington Country Store for that well-
   deserved ice cream, coffee, or pastry.

54.3 LEFT on Littleville Dam Rd. to the Gateway Regional
   High School. Congratulations on completing a tough but
   beautiful ride.

14

Peace Pagoda

Rating: Intermediate
Distance: 13, 14, 19 or 20 miles
Terrain: Flat to hilly
Towns: Leverett, Montague, Sunderland

Points of Interest: Leverett Town Center, Dakin Animal Shelter, Peace Pagoda, Leverett Sawmill

Description: Starting from Leverett Center, this is a 13-mile ride with options to make it longer appearing at the end of the directions below. Wherever started, the highlight of the ride is the Peace Pagoda in Leverett. A gravel driveway off Cave Hill Road leads up to the hilltop monument. A sign in the parking lot requests visitors to walk the last 0.3 mile. The monument is hidden from view by woods; then suddenly you come upon it. Constructed in 1985 by volunteers and the Nipponzan Myohoji monks, it is a monument to peace. Equipment, supplies, and food were all donated for its construction. Steps lead up to a balcony which surrounds the Pagoda, allowing a view of the various Buddhas as well as the surrounding countryside. Both the monument and the view are impressive. At the time of this writing, a new temple was in the process of being constructed. (The former temple burned to the ground.) A beautiful Japanese garden and pond are just below the site. A feeling of peace prevails here and should be respected by all visitors.

Directions:
START from the parking lot behind the Town Hall in
     Leverett Center. The Town Hall is beside the Post Office
     and across from the Congregational Church.

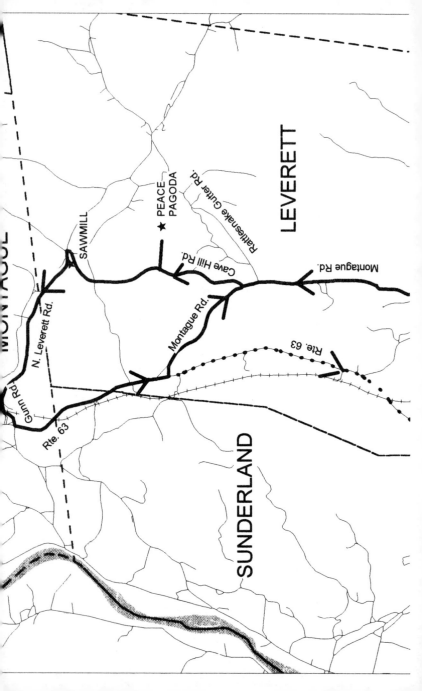

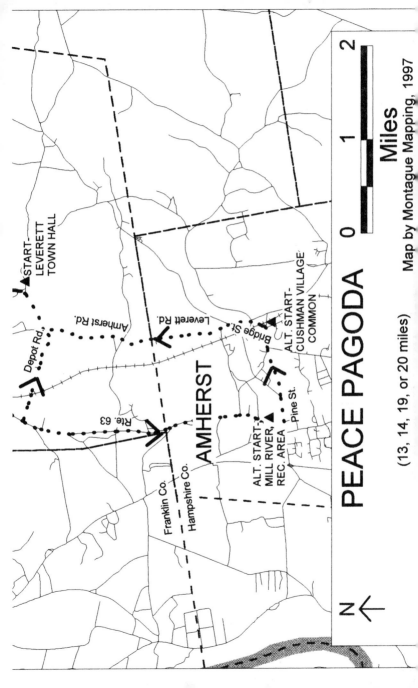

PEACE PAGODA

(13, 14, 19, or 20 miles)

START-
LEVERETT
TOWN HALL

Depot Rd.

Amherst Rd.

Leverett Rd.

Bridge St.

ALT. START-
CUSHMAN VILLAGE
COMMON

Pine St.

Rte. 63

AMHERST

ALT. START-
MILL RIVER,
REC. AREA

Franklin Co.
Hampshire Co.

N

Miles

0   1   2

Map by Montague Mapping, 1997

0.0 RIGHT onto Montague Rd. from the Town Hall and past Leverett Crafts and Arts.

0.8 PASS Leverett Elementary School on the right.

1.6 PASS the Dakin Animal Shelter on your right.

1.8 PASS Rattlesnake Gutter Rd. on your right.

2.0 RIGHT on Cave Hill Rd. and a long, gradual uphill climb. When the Peace Pagoda was dedicated, the celebrants walked up this road. You may want to walk it, too.

3.2 RIGHT at the crest of the hill past the mail box onto the gravel road leading up to the Peace Pagoda.

3.3 RIGHT into the parking lot. A sign explains that this is a "place to contemplate world peace as well as one's inner peace" and requests that you walk up the remaining 0.3 mile on foot.

3.4 The road on the left leads to the construction site for the Cambodian Temple, which is unrelated to the Peace Pagoda and its Japanese Buddhist Temple.

3.6 The old farmhouse on the left is the residence of the Nipponzan Myyohogi monks until their residence and temple are completed. At this point take the path to the right around the barrier and continue your uphill walk.

3.7 The Peace Pagoda greets you in all its reverence and beauty. Sit a few moments on one of the benches before walking up the steps and around the parapet to view the five Buddhas. Before descending, observe the beautiful view of the Mount Holyoke range and the valley below. Then walk around the pond and the Japanese garden. Finally, visit the construction site for the new residence and temple and read the explanatory sign. Linger a while, then go in peace.

4.1 RIGHT on Cave Hill Rd. Enjoy the long downhill.

5.1 LEFT on North Leverett Rd. into North Leverett. Pause at the old sawmill to observe the falls. Then follow the Sawmill River downhill to your next turn.

5.5 The house on your left at 29 North Leverett Rd. was formerly a wooden bucket factory. The owners have preserved some of the inner structure and have landscaped the grounds very attractively.

7.1 LEFT on Gunn Rd. immediately after the overpass. If you miss it, just take your next left onto Rte. 63.

7.3 LEFT on Rte. 63

8.5 The Robert Frost Hiking Trail Extension to Wendell State Forest crosses the road here exiting from Reservation Rd. and resuming at the Entering Leverett sign.

9.0 Pass the Craig Memorial Equestrian Center on your right with its beautiful pasture and horses in the foreground and a view of the Mount Toby range in the background.

9.2 LEFT on Montague Rd. (See *Option 1* below.)

10.6 BEAR RIGHT to stay on Montague Rd. and retrace your route from Cave Hill Rd. to Leverett Center.

12.6 LEFT into the Town Hall parking lot and end of ride.

OPTIONS FOR LONGER RIDES:

1. This option adds 1.5 miles. At milepoint 9.2 in the directions above, go STRAIGHT on Rte. 63 past Montague Road and past Long Hill Road. Take a LEFT onto Depot Rd. At the T-intersection, go LEFT. Then BEAR RIGHT, passing the other end of Long Hill Rd. Continue STRAIGHT to Leverett Center and the Town Hall.

2. This option adds 6.4 miles. START the ride from the Cushman Village Common on Pine and Bridge Streets in North Amherst. Park in the Common next to the railroad tracks. EXIT the Common at the north end. Turn RIGHT onto Bridge St. and cross the railroad tracks at an angle to avoid ensnaring your wheel. Cross over a bridge, pass State Street and turn LEFT onto Leverett Road which becomes Amherst Rd. in Leverett and Depot Road (where Depot Road enters on the left). Continue STRAIGHT, then bear RIGHT into Leverett Center. Retrace this route on return.

3. This option adds 7.3 miles. START at the Mill River Recreation Area in North Amherst. Go LEFT on Rte. 63 to the traffic lights and take a LEFT at the lights onto Pine St. and to Cushman Village. Go LEFT on Bridge Street. Cross the railroad tracks at a right angle to avoid ensnaring your wheel and follow the directions in Option 2 to Leverett Center. On your return, remain on Rte. 63 to the Mill River Recreation Area.

Whatever route you choose, peace be with you.

15

Poet's Seat ... and More

Rating: Novice to Intermediate
Distance: 33 miles, with options to shorten ride
Terrain: Mostly flat with one significant hill
Towns: Amherst, Sunderland, Montague, Greenfield, Leverett

Points of Interest: Sunderland Falls, Poet's Seat Tower, State Fish Hatchery, The Montague Mill

Description: Poets' Seat Tower sits on the top of a rocky ridge on Greenfield's highest point, offering an impressive view of the surrounding area. The site has always been popular with visitors and has inspired poets since the mid-19th century. A plaque on the tower reads, "Francis Goddard Tuckerman 1821-1871. This Greenfield resident was a gifted solitary poet much admired by Emerson, Hawthorne and Tennyson. Seeking solace in nature, he wrote verse and studied nature in Greenfield. The tower built in 1912 replaced a wooden tower built in 1873." Today the site continues to attract visitors, including bicyclists, who like the challenge of the uphill and the thrill of the downhill as well as the view from the top.

There are a number of ways to shorten this ride and still have a destination. Actually, the route is so lovely you don't need a destination. Just pedal as far as you please and turn around and retrace your path. If you prefer not to bicycle up the mountain, you can take a shortcut over to the Montague Mill or visit the falls in Sunderland or the Fish Hatchery in Montague. Options are listed in the directions. There's more to the ride than Poets' Seat.

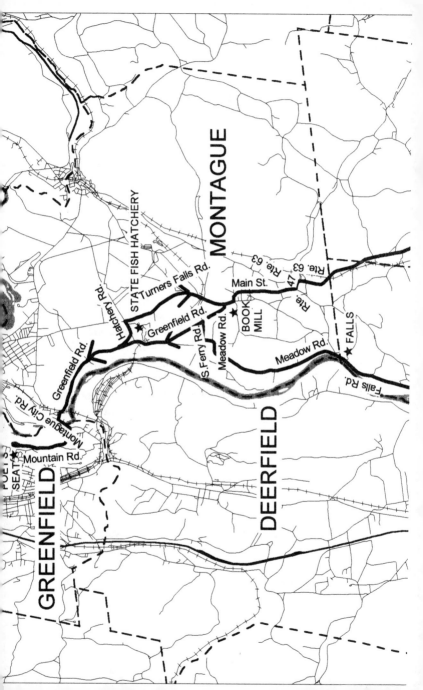

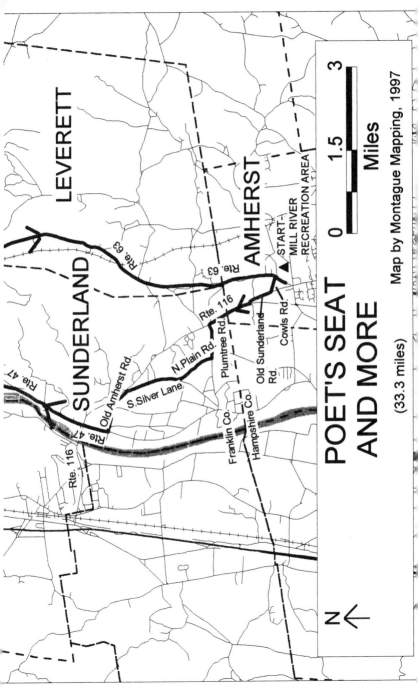

POET'S SEAT
AND MORE

(33.3 miles)

Map by Montague Mapping, 1997

Miles

0   1.5   3

N

LEVERETT

SUNDERLAND

AMHERST

Rte. 63

Rte. 63

Rte. 116

Rte. 47

Rte. 47

Rte. 116

Old Amherst Rd.

S. Silver Lane

N. Plain Rd.

Plumtree Rd.

Old Sunderland Rd.

Cowls Rd.

Franklin Co.

Hampshire Co.

START
MILL RIVER
RECREATION AREA

Directions:

START from the Mill River Recreation Area on Rte. 63 in the center of North Amherst.

0.0 RIGHT out of the driveway onto Rte. 63.

0.1 LEFT onto Cowls Rd. and past Cowls Lumber Yard.

0.4 RIGHT onto Old Sunderland Rd. Watch for the geese (both wild and domestic) at the pond on your right.

0.8 RIGHT onto Rte. 116 and past a fish farm on your left.

1.3 Entering Sunderland. Pass Bub's Barbecue, a popular spot and highly rated.

1.7 LEFT onto Plumtree Rd.

2.3 RIGHT onto North Plain Rd.

3.1 RIGHT on Silver Lane with views of the Mt. Toby range on the right.

4.1 LEFT onto Old Amherst Rd. Watch for the red-roofed Sunderland Elementary School and the view of Mt. Sugarloaf in the background.

4.9 RIGHT onto Rte. 47, Sunderland's attractive Main St. The Millstone Farm Market on your right has coffee, pastry, ice cream, fruit and snacks.

5.4 CROSS Rte. 116 at the lights and continue on Rte. 47. The Dairy Mart on your left has a restroom as well as refreshments.

5.6 Observe the giant sycamore on your left, one of the oldest trees in the Pioneer Valley.

6.8 LEFT onto Falls Rd. It may be bumpy but it's scenic and very popular with bicyclists.

8.5 Observe the falls on your right at the bridge and the Connecticut River on your left. You're on Meadow Rd. in Montague when you cross the bridge.

9.5 Pass the Smiarowski Farm on your right. Look for an asparagus stand there in the late spring.

10.2 Blue Meadow Farm on your right offers blue poppies and is popular with flower gardeners.

11.3 LEFT on South Ferry Rd. Ignore the *Bridge Closed* sign; Bicyclists can cross the bridge.

OPTION: You can shorten the ride here by taking Meadow
   Rd. to the Montague Mill and Blue Heron Cafe. Go
   right on Greenfield Rd. and you'll be there. Then continue
   the route by following directions at mile 23.5 below.
11.6 BEAR LEFT to stay on South Ferry Rd.
11.7 BEAR RIGHT to stay on South Ferry Rd.
12.3 LEFT on Greenfield Rd. (Here is another *OPTION* to
   shorten the ride; a right will take you over to Montague
   Mill and you can pick up the route at mile 29.5).
12.9 Pass Fish Hatchery Rd. (Here is another *OPTION* to
   shorten the ride by turning onto Fish Hatchery Rd.,
   taking it to the Fish Hatchery, and picking up the
   route at mile 21.4).
15.1 LEFT on Montague City Rd. and over the bridge into
   Greenfield.
15.4 RIGHT on Mountain Rd. and one mile uphill.
16.3 RIGHT at Poets' Seat and up to the Tower, but first
   look over the Greenfield Trails Council Trail Guide
   sign for Rocky Mountain and Highland Park at the
   entrance for an overview of the park. Warning: the
   road up is bumpy. Keep to the right at the
   intersection. It is not only smoother; its easier.
16.8 The Tower is located on a rocky lava ridge overlooking
   Greenfield and the Pioneer Valley. A panoramic view
   can be seen from the escarpment but a larger view is
   presented from the Tower. Bear right on the way down
   and take it easy; its very bumpy at this writing.
17.2 LEFT on Mountain Rd. and enjoy the downhill.
18.0 LEFT on Montague City Rd. and over the bridge back
   into the village of Montague City, town of Montague.
18.3 LEFT on Greenfield Rd. Continue to retrace the route.
20.2 LEFT on Greenfield Cross Rd. for the Fish Hatchery, or
   OPTION: remain on Greenfield Rd. to Montague Mill.
20.6 LEFT on Hatchery Rd. from Greenfield Cross Rd.
20.8 RIGHT into the State Fish Hatchery along an avenue of
   cathedral pines. Visiting hours are 9 to 3.

21.1 Sign: "No Vehicles/Bikes Beyond This Point." On the
    left is a parking area, a picnic table and stairs down
    to the hatchery. Take a walk and observe the fish at
    their various stages of development, then return to
    your locked bicycle and bike back out to the road.
21.4 RIGHT on Hatchery Rd.
21.5 RIGHT on Turners Falls Rd.
23.5 RIGHT on Greenfield Rd. to stop at the Montague
    Mill and Blue Heron Cafe. To continue, cross over the
    bridge into the village of Montague Center.
23.7 BEAR LEFT on Main St.
23.8 BEAR RIGHT at the Common and through this
    classic New England village. Pass the Post Office on the
    left and the Montague Mini Market on the right.
24.1 Read the kiosk on your right for directions.
24.9 LEFT on Rte. 47.
25.1 RIGHT on Rte. 63.
26.3 Pass Reservation Rd. and Mt. Toby State Forest.
26.4 Entering Leverett. Pass the Robert Frost Trail
    Extension to Wendell St. Forest on your left.
26.7 Pass the footpath to Cranberry Pond on your right.
26.8 Pass the Craig Memorial Equestrian Center and observe
    the excellent view of the Mt. Toby Range on the right.
33.3 LEFT into the Mill River Recreation Area and end of the
    ride. If time, energy and weather permit, take a hike,
    go for a swim, or flop on the grass and relax.

16

Quabbin Loop

Rating: Intermediate
Distance: 20 miles
Terrain: Flat to hilly
Towns: Belchertown, Ware

Points of Interest: Quabbin Reservoir, Summit and Visitors' Center; Winsor Dam, Enfield Lookout, Goodnough Dike

Description: This is the shorter of two rides listed in this book which feature the Quabbin Reservoir. The other one (Ride 18) encircles and includes it; this one goes directly to it, does a loop within it and goes only a little beyond it before returning to the start. The Quabbin Reservoir was created about sixty years ago in order to provide drinking water for Boston by flooding the Swift River Valley, including the towns of Dana, Enfield, Prescott, and Greenwich. The project created also a beautiful park and an "accidental wilderness." Although short, this is a hilly ride, but not steep. It is possible to skip some of the hills, shorten the ride, and still enjoy the park. It is also possible to park just past the Visitors' Center and just do the inside loop. The options are listed below.

Directions:
START from the Crystal Spring Market Place at the junction of Route 202 and Route 9 in Belchertown. Leave the parking area at the exit opposite CVS and McDonald's.
0.0 LEFT onto Rte. 202 and right at the lights onto Rte. 9. This is rural countryside but becomes wooded as you near Quabbin Reservoir.
3.1 LEFT at the Winsor Dam-Quabbin Reservoir sign into Quabbin Park.

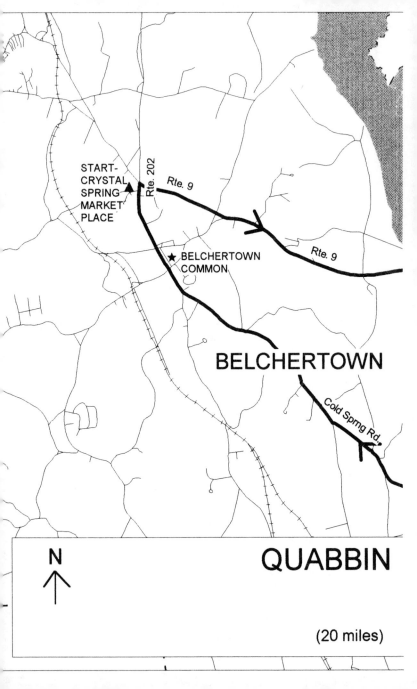

START-
CRYSTAL
SPRING
MARKET
PLACE

Rte. 202

Rte. 9

Rte. 9

★ BELCHERTOWN
COMMON

BELCHERTOWN

Cold Sprng Rd.

N

QUABBIN

(20 miles)

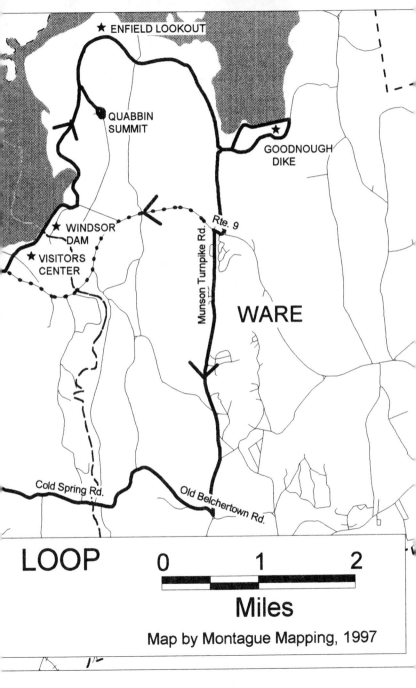

★ ENFIELD LOOKOUT

● QUABBIN
SUMMIT

★ GOODNOUGH
DIKE

Rte. 9

★ WINDSOR
DAM

★ VISITORS
CENTER

Munson Turnpike Rd.

WARE

Cold Spring Rd.

Old Belchertown Rd.

LOOP

0   1   2

Miles

Map by Montague Mapping, 1997

3.5 STOP at the Visitors' Center on your right. Look at the "before and after" pictures and other exhibits. Use the rest rooms and fill your water bottles, if necessary.

3.7 CROSS Winsor Dam. Built in 1940, it is 2,640 feet long and 170 feet high. BEAR LEFT past the rotary and over the spillway bridge.

4.2 PASS the sign "To Quabbin Summit Tower" on your right and observe the 400-foot spillway on your left. A gradual uphill begins.

4.9 PASS Winsor Memorial Park on your left. Frank E. Winsor was the Chief Engineer of the Metropolitan District Water Supply Commission. A monument and two stone benches were erected here in his honor. The view may be overgrown.

5.6 A pullout affords a better view of the Reservoir.

5.7 RIGHT to the Summit Tower.

6.1 RIGHT up the path to the Tower.

6.2 The summit and the tower provide a beautiful view of the surrounding area. Spend as much time as you like here, then go back down the path to the road.

6.3 RIGHT past the Rest Rooms, around the rotary, and then downhill.

6.8 BEAR RIGHT at the Rotary towards Goodnough Dike.

7.3 STOP at Enfield Lookout for the most beautiful view in the Park. It overlooks the former site of the Town of Enfield. Bald eagles are frequently seen from here.

8.0 Open fields provide a break in the woods and an opportunity to walk down to the water and along the shore via a path on the left.

9.4 LEFT for an optional two-mile loop to Goodnough Dike, which you can see from the road as you approach the area. The loop involves a moderate climb either way you go. You can also ride in for a beautiful view of the reservoir and then reverse direction. However, the view of the dike from below is quite impressive. If you choose this *OPTION*, add two miles to the ride.

10.2 RIGHT to Rte. 9. (*OPTION*: To shorten the ride, take
     Rte. 9 back to the start). To continue the official route:
10.3 LEFT on Munson Turnpike Rd. After a cemetery on
     your left and a trailer park on your right, this road is
     mainly rural residential and leads to a more scenic road.
12.7 BEAR RIGHT here.
13.2 RIGHT on Old Belchertown Rd. The short, steep hill
     flattens out very soon. You'll enjoy this lovely road.
13.5 BEAR RIGHT and stay on Old Belchertown Rd. Take it
     easy on the curves on the downhill to enjoy the scenery.
15.0 CROSS the Swift River on a partially barricaded bridge
     onto Cold Spring Road. Continue straight through the
     Swift River Wildlife Management Area on a gentle
     uphill.
16.2 BEAR RIGHT at a grassy triangle and continue on Cold
     Springs Road.
16.6 OBSERVE Cold Spring on the right in an orchard. A
     sign provides information. Belchertown was originally
     called Cold Spring.
17.0 RIGHT on Rte. 181 and downhill.
19.4 PASS Belchertown Common.
20.3 LEFT into the Crystal Springs Market Place parking
     lot. End of the ride.

17

Rattlesnake Gutter

Rating: Intermediate for Rattlesnake Gutter Loop
and Novice for Puffer's Pond Loop
Distance: 10 or 19 miles
Terrain: Flat to hilly, two gravel roads
Towns: Leverett, Amherst

Points of Interest: Leverett Center, Dakin Animal Shelter,
coke kiln, Saw Mill River Falls, Village Co-op, Rattlesnake
Gutter, Cushman Village Store, Puffer's Pond

Description: Rattlesnake Gutter, the main feature of this ride,
is a wonderfully scenic area with a gravel road running
parallel to a small ravine or "gutter" which was formed by the
endwash or spillway of a glacial lake. Lovely woods climb up
one side of the road and spectacular cliffs on the other. The
road is gravel but it is rideable with a road bike. However,
since it drops off rather steeply on the "gutter" side, it should
be ridden with care and you may want to walk parts of it. It is
uphill from both ends, but easier to bicycle from Moore's
Corner than Leverett Center. Even if you prefer athletics to
aesthetics, pause to appreciate the beauty and go slow on the
downhill. Everyone who has ridden (or walked) this road has
loved it. It is beautiful and unique and truly one of Leverett's
treasures. It is popular year round with walkers, and since it
is closed to traffic in the winter, with skiers and snowshoers
also. When it's open it is used by car drivers as a short cut
between Montague Road and North Leverett Road, so beware
of the occasional auto. The ride includes two loops: the
Rattlesnake Gutter loop and the Puffer's Pond loop. They may
be ridden separately or together and both can be ridden in
reverse or modified as explained in the directions that follow.

Directions:

START from the parking lot behind the Town Hall in
   Leverett Center.

0.0 RIGHT from the driveway between the Town Hall and
   the Post Office onto Montague Rd. and past Leverett
   Crafts and Arts, formerly a box factory.

1.8 PASS Rattlesnake Gutter Rd. on your right. You'll come
   down this road later in the ride.

1.9 RIGHT on Cave Hill Rd. -- 1.3 miles of gradual uphill
   followed by 0.5 mile of downhill. (*OPTION*: To avoid the
   uphill but lengthen the ride, stay on Montague Rd., go
   right on Rte. 63, right on North Leverett Rd., and right on
   Rattlesnake Gutter Rd. to the Village Co-op. See mile 5.8
   below)

3.2 Arrive at the top of Cave Hill Rd. just after a mailbox and
   before a downhill sign. Pass the driveway to the Peace
   Pagoda on your right. (See Ride 14 for details on Pagoda).

3.7 RIGHT on Hemenway Rd., a woodsy, hard-packed
   country road.

5.0 PASS Old Coke Kiln Rd. Continue on Hemenway Rd.

5.3 Observe the old coke kiln on your left but don't
   venture inside; it's unsafe. Charcoal production was a
   Leverett industry until the 1970s.

5.3 BEAR LEFT on Old Mill Yard Road just past the coke
   kiln.

5.4 STOP on the bridge and look upstream at photogenic
   Saw Mill River Falls, then continue but keep towards the
   middle to avoid soft gravel and a dropoff as you round
   the corner and go uphill. Better yet, walk it.

5.5 LEFT on Rattlesnake Gutter Rd. past a cemetery and
   the Sawmill River on your right.

5.8 STOP at the Village Co-op on your left for refreshments
   and restrooms. They have great pastry, pizza, homemade
   soup, hot and cold beverages, and more.

5.8 Go RIGHT out of the parking lot back onto Rattlesnake
   Gutter Rd. in the direction from which you just came.

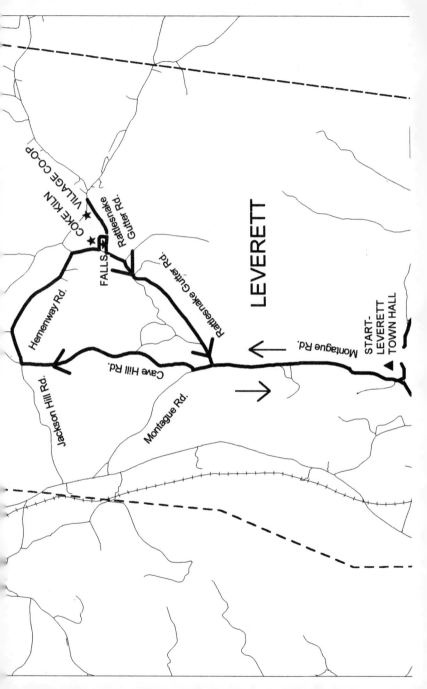

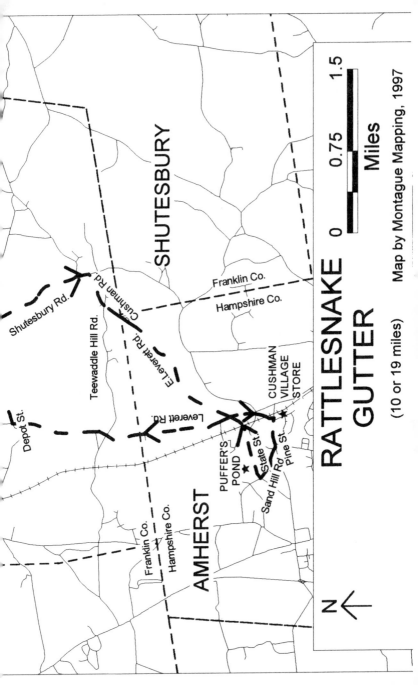

RATTLESNAKE GUTTER

(10 or 19 miles)

Map by Montague Mapping, 1997

Miles

0   0.75   1.5

N

SHUTESBURY

Shutesbury Rd.

Cushman Rd.

Teewaddle Hill Rd.

Eleverett Rd.

Depot St.

Leverett Rd.

Franklin Co.
Hampshire Co.

Franklin Co.
Hampshire Co.

AMHERST

PUFFER'S POND

State St.

Sand Hill Rd

Pine St.

CUSHMAN VILLAGE STORE

6.3 STOP on the bridge and observe the top of the falls as it tumbles down over the rocks -- then onward and upward. Notice the white blazes on the trees where the Metacomet-Monadnock Hiking Trail comes through "the Gutter." The double blaze signifies a turn for hikers.

7.0 STOP at the top to observe the cliffs on your right. Look for the "ruby lips." Continue slowly down the road. Observe "the gutter" on your right but don't ride too near the edge. Keep toward the middle of the road. Dismount for traffic to be safe.

8.0 LEFT on Montague Rd. and retrace your route to Leverett Center.

9.8 LEFT into the driveway between the Leverett Town Hall and Post Office. *OPTION: This* is the end of the short ride. Continue as follows for the Puffer's Pond loop:

9.9 LEFT on Shutesbury Rd. at the grassy triangle.

11.3 STRAIGHT onto Cushman Rd. and across Roaring Brook

11.5 BEAR RIGHT on Cushman Rd., which will become East Leverett Rd. in Amherst and leads to Cushman Village.

11.8 Teewaddle Hill on your right is a scenic gravel road that cuts over to Amherst Rd. and may be used to shorten the ride extension. (*OPTION:* A right on Amherst Rd. at four corners and straight on Depot Rd. will bring you back to Leverett Center). GO STRAIGHT to continue the Puffer's Pond loop. Watch for the Highland cattle as you pass a farm ahead on your right.

13.5 Leverett Rd. is on your right. (*OPTION:* Taking this road brings you back towards Leverett Center and shortens the route. It becomes Amherst Rd. in Leverett then Depot Rd. and Montague Rd.) GO STRAIGHT to continue the Puffer's Pond loop.

13.6 CROSS the bridge over Cushman Brook at Mill River Conservation Area (not to be confused with the Mill River Recreation Area) and the Robert Frost Trail crossing.

13.9 CAUTION: Cross the R.R. tracks at an angle to avoid ensnaring your wheel. You may want to stop and snack at the Cushman Village Store on your left opposite the Common. Otherwise BEAR RIGHT on Pine St. for a refreshing downhill to State Street.

14.7 RIGHT on State Street.

15.1 STOP SIGN -- cross Sand Hill Rd. and continue on State Street to Puffer's Pond for a swim or a rest stop. There's an outhouse but no dressing room. Swimming, fishing and canoeing are all permitted, but there is no lifeguard. Don't be confused by a sign that says Factory Hollow Pond -- that's the official name, but the natives call it Puffer's.

15.8 LEFT and LEFT again onto Leverett Rd., which you passed previously.

16.6 Pass the right of way to the Eastman Brook Conservation Area.

17.9 STRAIGHT on Depot Rd., which comes in from the left. BEAR RIGHT towards Leverett Center. Pass Leverett Pond which the summer people call Echo Lake. Depot Road ends and Montague Rd. begins at the grassy triangle at Shutesbury Rd. (*OPTION:* To avoid the short, steep pitch on Montague Rd., you can turn right here, then left at the Stop Sign and back to Montague Rd.)

18.6 RIGHT into the Town Hall parking lot for the end of the longer ride. If you didn't do so earlier, look at the painting and map on the front of the Town Hall and the sculpture entitled "Conversation" in the front yard.

18

Roundabout the Quabbin

Rating: Advanced
Distance: 62 miles
Terrain: Hilly
Towns: Belchertown, Pelham, Shutesbury, New Salem,
Petersham, Hardwick, Ware

Points of Interest: Belchertown Common, Historic Pelham
Town Hall Complex, Quabbin Reservoir, New Salem Center,
Petersham Common, Hardwick Common and General Store,
Quabbin Park, Goodnough Dike, Enfield Lookout, Quabbin
Summit, Winsor Dam, Quabbin Visitors' Center

Description: This is a long, hilly ride, but it can be delightful
if done at a comfortable pace with adequate rest stops in cool
weather. This beautiful route circles around the Quabbin
Reservoir, giving occasional views of the water, and traveling
through woods, up and down hills, past fields, farms and old
stone walls, and into small towns with classic New England
commons. Near the end, the ride enters Quabbin Park for a
close-up view of the Reservoir, which was created to provide
clean drinking water for Boston. About sixty years ago, the
towns of Dana, Enfield, Prescott, and Greenwich were
obliterated by damming the Swift River and Beaver Brook. As
the Swift River Valley was flooded, the mountains became
islands, and an "accidental wilderness" was created. The area
was opened in 1952 for limited recreation, and it is now
visited by hundreds of thousands of people each year, including fishermen, hikers, hunters, picnickers, bird-watchers
and bicyclists. The mileage given in the following directions
is approximate. For a shorter Quabbin route, see Ride 16.

Directions: START from the parking lot at the South end of Belchertown Common (intersection Rtes. 202, 21, 181).

0.0 LEFT out of the parking lot and left at the North end of the Common towards Rte. 202.

0.2 RIGHT onto Rte. 202 North through a residential area to the intersection of Rtes. 202 and 9 at Crystal Springs Market Place.

0.9 STRAIGHT across Route 9. Continue on Rte. 202 and begin a gentle 10-mile climb through alternating wooded and residential countryside.

2.5 Open meadows replace the woods, but the woods reappear and disappear, as do occasional residences.

3.2 Pass Jabish Brook Conservation Area on the right.

4.4 Pelham Town Line.

5.4 Gate No. 8 on the right is a fishing access to Quabbin Reservoir.

8.4 The Historic Pelham Town Hall Complex, a Massachusetts Historic Landmark, is on the left at the corner of Amherst Rd. The Town Hall dates back to 1743, the oldest in continuous use in New England. It is worth stopping to read the sign, view the buildings and visit the old cemetery out back.

8.6 A small general store is on the left.

9.0 PULL OVER at a descriptive sign and a long stone wall for a distant view of Quabbin Reservoir and the surrounding countryside. Continuing the ride, the terrain will become rolling and the woods block the view.

10.2 Shutesbury Town Line.

12.7 PASS the road to Shutesbury Center and Lake Wyola on your left, unless you want to take a side trip uphill.

13.4 New Salem Town Line.

14.2 Cross Shutesbury Town Line again. You'll be back in New Salem in a minute.

16.6 Hamilton Orchards is 0.25 mile up the road on your left, a potential refreshment stop (fruit, pastry, coffee).

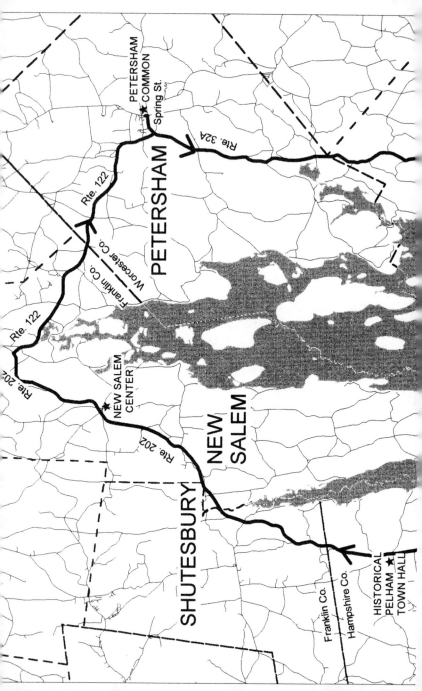

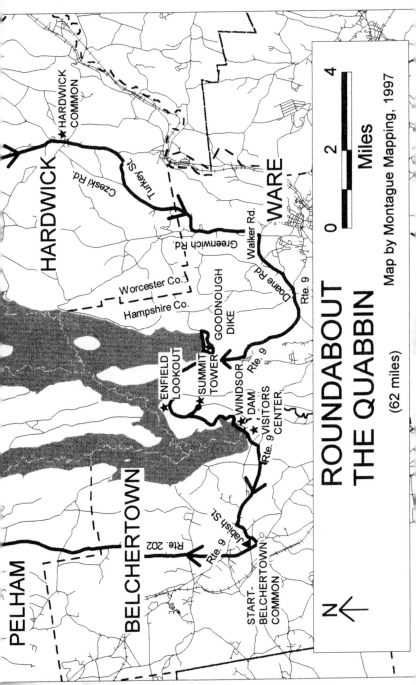

ROUNDABOUT THE QUABBIN

(62 miles)

Map by Montague Mapping, 1997

Miles

0   2   4

N

PELHAM

BELCHERTOWN

HARDWICK

★ HARDWICK COMMON

Czeski Rd.

Turkey St.

Greenwich Rd.

Walker Rd.

WARE

Worcester Co.
Hampshire Co.

GOODNOUGH DIKE

Doane Rd.

Rte. 9

★ ENFIELD LOOKOUT

★ SUMMIT TOWER

★ WINDSOR DAM

Rte. 9

★ VISITORS CENTER

Rte. 9

Rte. 202

Rte. 9

Jabish St.

START- BELCHERTOWN COMMON

17.9 A road on your right leads a short way in to New Salem Center, a well-preserved, classic New England village worth visiting. The New Salem General Store and Restaurant are on the left on 202. New Salem is at the height of land, so a long downhill follows. The road shoulder is too narrow for use.

18.5 PULL OVER for a view on your right, then continue downhill.

20.8 A road on your right leads to the Swift River Historical Society (open from 2 to 4 P.M., Wed. and Sun. in July & August, and Sun. only, Sept. through mid Oct.)

21.2 RIGHT on Rte. 122 towards Petersham. The road shoulder is gravel here. Ride out on the road.

22.2 The Reservoir is in view on your right.

22.6 Gate 31 provides access to the Reservoir and a good stopping place if you're interested.

23.6 South Spectacle Pond is on your right and North Spectacle Pond is on your left.

24.9 Petersham Town Line. You're in Worcester County now. Pass the Federated Women's Clubs State Forest on your right. Enjoy cycling the rolling hills on 122.

27.2 Pass Brooks Pond on your left.

28.8 LEFT at the light onto Hardwick Road.

29.0 RIGHT at the Y onto Spring Street at the Post Office.

29.3 LEFT at the Stop sign.

29.5 The Country Store opposite the Petersham Common includes a restaurant and a rest room. After a rest stop, reverse direction and go south on Main Street.

29.7 RIGHT on Spring Street.

30.0 LEFT at the Y onto Hardwick Road at the Post Office.

30.2 STRAIGHT at the light onto Rte. 32A. This is a pretty country road lined with old stone walls. The woods change to fields interspersed with old and new houses. A downhill leads to an up.

32.7 BEAR RIGHT at the Y intersection and go downhill on Rte. 32A. Old stone walls and woods continue.

35.1 Hardwick Town Line. This pretty road continues with woods, walls, fields, occasional houses, and rolling hills.

39.6 BEAR RIGHT just past the Gate 43 fishing access to the Reservoir and remain on Rte. 32A.

40.1 Hardwick Center with Common and General Store provides another opportunity for rest and refreshment before going uphill on Rte. 32A.

41.3 BEAR RIGHT at the yellow directional sign onto Turkey Street (unmarked at this writing) -- an uphill. This is a very curved road with lots of ups and downs.

42.5 LEFT where Czeski Road intersects and then continue downhill on Turkey Street. Be careful not to go off the edge of the blacktop. Enjoy the countryside but be prepared for the curves and bumps on this downhill.

45.0 LEFT at the T intersection onto Greenwich Rd., which is unmarked. (Campbell Rd. is across the intersection). Stay on the road with the double yellow lines. Watch for:

46.8 SHARP RIGHT on Walker Road and downshift as soon as you see it. It's a short, steep, narrow, bumpy uphill, but also a shortcut that avoids downtown Ware.

47.5 STRAIGHT across Osborne Rd. and remain on Walker Road. This section of the road is much smoother.

48.2 RIGHT at the T intersection onto Doane Rd. and downhill.

48.6 RIGHT at another T intersection onto Rte. 9 at the Congregational Meeting House and uphill. You're out of the woods and on a smooth paved shoulder now.

51.2 RIGHT into Quabbin Park and Reservation.

52.1 RIGHT toward Goodnough Dike.

52.3 RIGHT at the Y intersection and downhill.

52.7 Look up! The Dike is on your left. Follow the road up and around the rotary, then across the dike. Look right! There's Quabbin Reservoir in all its glory.

53.5 BEAR RIGHT at the rotary and skirt the Reservoir.

53.9 RIGHT at the T intersection.

54.0 RIGHT at the Y intersection towards Winsor Dam.

55.5 The woods give way to fields on your right.

56.2 Stop at Enfield Lookout on your right for the best view in the Park where you can search the sky for eagles.

56.6 RIGHT at the rotary and right towards Winsor Dam, or if you have the energy for another hill, go left to the Summit Tower, then reverse direction and return to this point. The side trip adds a mile.

57.4 Pass Winsor Memorial Park on your right and continue downhill.

57.9 The Spillway will be on your right. It's impressive when it's filled with water.

58.1 RIGHT towards Winsor Dam.

58.2 RIGHT around the rotary and across the Dam.

58.8 STOP at the Visitors' Center, see the exhibits, use the rest rooms, fill your water bottle.

59.2 RIGHT at the T intersection onto Rte. 9 towards Belchertown

61.3 LEFT onto Jabish St. (Rte. 21).

61.4 Cross Jabish Brook.

62.1 Arrive back at the Belchertown Common and the end of the ride.

19

Rowe Roundabout

Rating: Intermediate to Advanced
Distance: 38 miles
Terrain: Hilly
Towns: Charlemont, Rowe, Monroe and Florida,
Massachusetts; Whitingham and Readsboro, Vermont

Points of Interest: Deerfield River, Pelham Brook and Lake,
Whitingham Common and Park, Brigham Young Monument,
Brown's General Store, Readsboro General Store, Monroe
Bridge, Yankee Atomic Power Plant, Bear Swamp Visitors'
Center, Hoosac Tunnel, Zoar Gap Rapids

Description: This ride strays out of the Pioneer Valley into
Vermont and the Berkshires. It begins in Charlemont along
the banks of the Deerfield River, then follows Pelham Brook
up to Pelham Lake in Rowe. Historic markers in sleepy little
Rowe indicate that it once nourished several industries. Even
the Yankee Atomic Plant is now out of commission and Rowe
is very quiet. You'll pass many points of interest on this ride,
including the Brigham Young Monument which honors the
prominent Mormon leader who was born in Vermont. You
may want to stop in the town of Monroe Bridge and watch the
canoeists and kayakers putting in on this Class IV stretch of
river. The Bear Swamp Visitors' Center just down the road
offers exhibits and sanitary facilities. Another worthwhile
stop is the Hoosac Tunnel in Florida, which was the longest
tunnel in North America until 1916 and is still the longest
tunnel east of the Mississippi River. A final point of interest
is the Zoar Gap Rapids where you can view the excitement as
canoeists and kayakers run the rapids when the water's up.

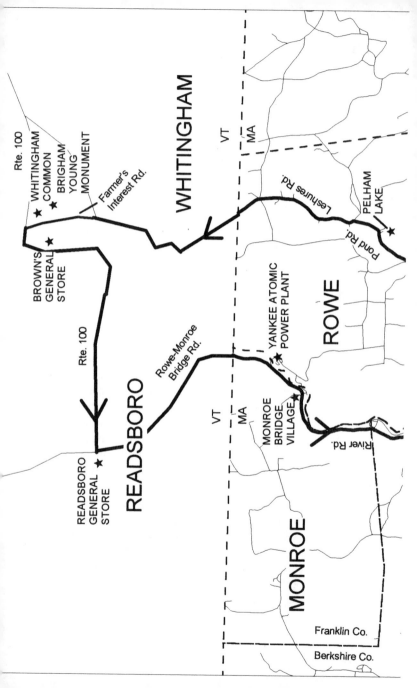

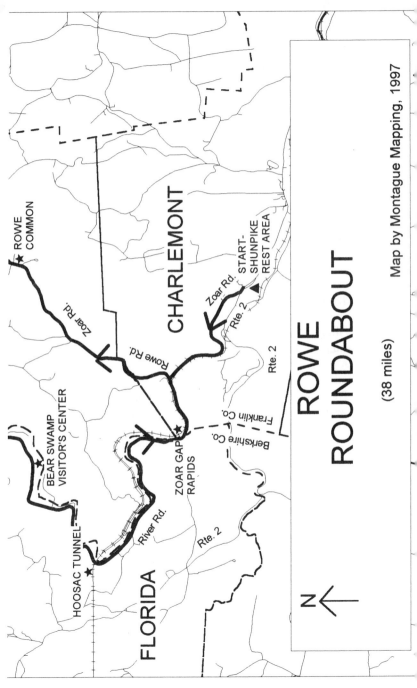

ROWE ROUNDABOUT

(38 miles)

Map by Montague Mapping, 1997

N

ROWE COMMON

CHARLEMONT

Zoar Rd.

START-SHUNPIKE REST AREA

Rte. 2

Zoar Rd.

Rowe Rd.

Franklin Co.

Berkshire Co.

BEAR SWAMP VISITOR'S CENTER

ZOAR GAP RAPIDS

River Rd.

Rte. 2

HOOSAC TUNNEL

FLORIDA

Directions:

START from the Shunpike Roadside Rest Area on Rte. 2 along the Deerfield River, located two miles from the center of Charlemont (or 1.4 miles from Rte. 8A South at the west end of town, or 0.2 miles from Zoar Road).

0.0 LEFT out of the parking area onto Rte. 2.

0.2 RIGHT on Zoar Rd. and along the Deerfield River.

2.7 RIGHT on Rowe Rd. at the junction before the underpass. Leave the river. Do not go under the underpass. Pelham Brook will be on your right as you pedal a long uphill to Rowe and on to Vermont.

3.4 ENTER ROWE and watch for signposts indicating former industries.

4.7 The road on your left is a shortcut to Monroe Bridge. No guarantees as to road conditions. A sign indicates Yankee Atomic Visitors' Center but the plant itself is closed.

6.0 On your right is the Community Church, Museum and Village School. Signs for a wagon shop, casket shop, and boot shop appear on the left and right.

6.3 A pretty place to pause is the site of the former Bullard Sawmill and a mill pond on your right.

6.4 The Rowe Common and the Town Hall follow. There's a gazebo down by the pond and a small picnic shelter across the street.

6.5 BEAR RIGHT on Pond Road. Signs for the Browning Bench Tool Factory appear on both the left and the right.

7.0 Observe the site of Fort Pelham on your left.

7.2 Beautiful Pelham Lake is on your right.

7.3 The Town Beach is down the gravel road on your right, opposite the Rowe School. Privies and a water pump are available. Add 0.2 mile if you go down and back. Back en route, you pass Pelham Lake Park, a wooded area with picnic tables, on your right.

7.7 BEAR LEFT or straight on Leshure Road. (No sign)

7.8 BEAR RIGHT or straight on Leshure Road.

10.1 VERMONT LINE: The road continues uphill a short way before flattening out and going downhill. Enjoy the views.

13.1 STRAIGHT on Farmers Interest Road.

13.4 LEFT at the T intersection.

13.8 Whitingham Common and Park on your right is a good place to stop and rest. There are picnic tables and an outhouse. The Brigham Young monument overlooks the ball field behind the picnic area. A playground and shelter are across the street.

13.9 LEFT on Rte. 100 from Farmers Interest Road. CAUTION: steep downhill followed by a sharp turn and more downhill. Pass Sadawga Pond on your left.

14.5 SHARP LEFT and continue downhill on Rte. 100.

15.0 Brown's General Store in Whitingham is a potential stop but you're on a downhill so watch for it on your left. The south end of Harriman Reservoir will be on your right. The terrain will be mostly downhill to Readsboro. In fact, it will be mostly downhill for the rest of the ride.

20.3 LEFT onto Rowe-Monroe Bridge Road in Readsboro just over the bridge and past the gazebo. Readsboro General Store will be on your right and is a recommended stop. The Deerfield River will be on your left and will escort you for the remainder of the ride, although it is not always in sight.

22.6 There is a picnic area and a privy near the Deerfield River on your left.

23.0 The closed Yankee Atomic Power Plant appears on your left. At mile 23.5, you are directly opposite it.

24.3 VILLAGE OF MONROE BRIDGE. Take a left for a short (0.5 mile) side trip down to the bridge to observe the Class IV whitewater during a water release. Back on the main road, stop and look through the trees at the roaring river and the "hotshot" canoeists and kayakers.

26.5 FLORIDA TOWN LINE. You're in Berkshire County.

26.6 Dunbar Brook Picnic Area on your left leads to the takeout for the Class IV boaters (worth a stop).

27.4 Bear Swamp Visitors' Center is on your left, with flush
toilets, drinking fountain, and exhibits.

29.4 A road on your left leads to the put-in for the Class 2
Section of the Deerfield River leading to a Class 3
drop known as the Zoar Gap Rapids, which is fun to
watch when there's a water release.

30.5 The Hoosac Tunnel is on your right. It connects
Florida and North Adams. Walk in and take a look but
watch out and listen for trains.

34.0 Zoar Gap Rapids is on your left. Stop and watch the
canoeists, kayakers and rafts come through. There's
bound to be a spill or two.

34.3 After crossing the bridge, the Zoar Picnic Area with
picnic tables and outhouses is on your right. Here
also is the put-in for a Class 1 section of the river.

35.0 CAUTION: Go through the underpass with care. Keep
to the far right and give a hoot!

35.2 PASS Rowe Road on your left (a previous turn at
mile 2.7) and continue straight, retracing your route along
the Deerfield River to the ride start.

37.6 LEFT on Rte. 2.

37.7 RIGHT into the Shunpike Roadside Rest Area. You have
completed the Rowe Roundabout. Try it in reverse some
time. It's great either way.

OPTION: An alternative route from either direction is to bear
right on Rte. 100 at Whitingham Common, take Rte. 100
to Jacksonville, stop at the General Store, pick up Route
112, stop at the North River Winery, continue on 112 to
Rte. 8A to Charlemont, then Rte. 2 back to the Shunpike
Roadside Rest Area.

21

Station to Station

Rating: Novice to Intermediate
Distance: 16 miles
Terrain: Flat to rolling (mostly flat)
Towns: Amherst, Belchertown, Hadley

Points of Interest: Harvey Allen Trail; Lawrence Swamp, Elf Meadow, Holyoke Range, Sweet Alice Conservation Area, Atkins Farms Fruit Bowl, Norwottuck Rail Trail

Description: This route goes by some of Amherst's numerous conservation areas and gives cyclists an opportunity to get off their bikes and go for a short hike. It is a short, easy ride which begins and ends at Station Road in South Amherst. Starting at the Norwottuck Rail Trail parking area, it crosses Station Road to the Harvey Allen Trail, which is an extension of the Norwottuck Rail Trail to Warren Wright Road in Belchertown. From Warren Wright Road the route turns onto Orchard Street, which becomes Hulst Road in Amherst. At Bay Road it heads towards Atkins Farms Fruit Bowl, a favorite refreshment and pit stop for bikers, then continues on into Hadley. There it turns onto Moody Bridge Road, then onto South Maple Street, and finally the Norwottuck Rail Trail back to Station Road. There are also options to shorten the ride and to eliminate hills. For more information about the Rail Trail itself, see *Great Rail-Trails of the Northeast* (listed in References, page 167).

Directions:
START at the Station Road parking lot for the Norwottuck Rail-Trail in South Amherst, near the Lawrence Swamp Conservation Area.

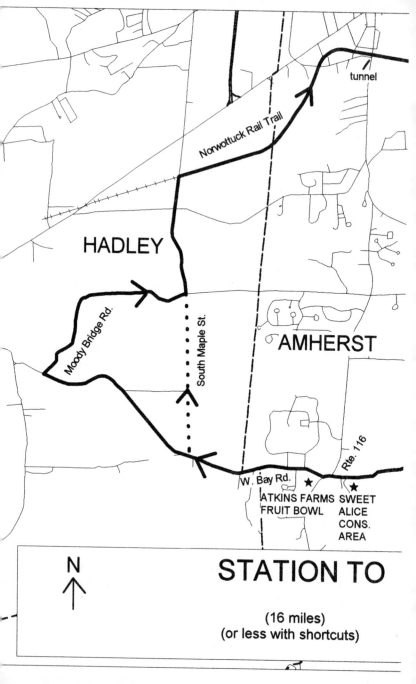

Norwottuck Rail Trail

tunnel

HADLEY

Moody Bridge Rd.

South Maple St.

AMHERST

Rte. 116

W. Bay Rd.

ATKINS FARMS
FRUIT BOWL ★

SWEET
ALICE
CONS.
AREA ★

N

STATION TO

(16 miles)
(or less with shortcuts)

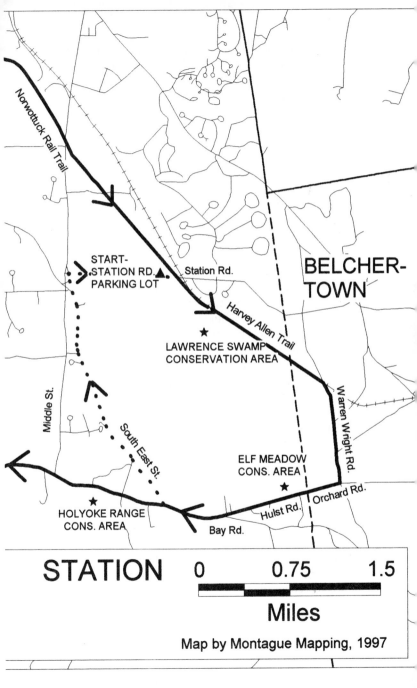

Norwottuck Rail Trail

START-
STATION RD.
PARKING LOT

Station Rd.

BELCHER-
TOWN

Harvey Allen Trail

★
LAWRENCE SWAMP
CONSERVATION AREA

Middle St.

South East St.

Warren Wright Rd.

ELF MEADOW
CONS. AREA
★

★
HOLYOKE RANGE
CONS. AREA

Hulst Rd.

Orchard Rd.

Bay Rd.

STATION   0   0.75   1.5

Miles

Map by Montague Mapping, 1997

0.0 STRAIGHT across Station Rd. onto Harvey Allen Trail, an extension of the Norwottuck Rail Trail into Belchertown. It parallels the Lawrence Swamp Conservation Area and hiking trails.

1.4 RIGHT onto Warren Wright Rd. from the parking area at the end of the extension.

2.2 RIGHT on Orchard Road, which becomes Hulst Rd. in Amherst.

2.6 PASS Elf Meadow Conservation Area on your left. This land has a large population of climbing (or "Hartford") fern. The 1.4 mile Brookfield Trail starts on the west side of Elf Meadow and goes north and west to Southeast Street. You can lock your bike and take a walk.

3.2 RIGHT on Bay Road.

3.7 PASS Southeast Street on your right, which is a possible shortcut back to Station Road for a very short ride.

4.4 PASS Holyoke Range Conservation Area on your left. This 130-acre tract of land has numerous hiking trails, including the Robert Frost Trail. You can hike to the Horse Caves or Rattlesnake Knob.

4.7 PASS Middle Street on your right, which is another possible shortcut back to Station Rd.

5.5 PASS Sweet Alice Conservation Area on your left. This 41-acre tract of land includes orchards, open fields, woods and a stream.

5.7 LEFT on West St. (Rte. 116)

5.8 RIGHT on West Bay Road and left into Atkins Farms for a meal, a snack, a pit stop or shopping. Go STRAIGHT if you prefer not to stop. Go LEFT onto West Bay Road if you do stop.

7.1 PASS South Maple Street, which is a shortcut to the Norwottuck Rail Trail if you wish to shorten the ride.

8.6 RIGHT on Moody Bridge Rd. and downhill on this curving country road. A short uphill follows and then the route becomes flat for the rest of the ride.

9.4 The road changes to hard-surface gravel but its good bicycling and will change to pavement shortly. Bri-Mar Stables is on your left. A panoramic view of the mountains is on your right.

10.2 LEFT on South Maple Street. Watch for speeding traffic on this narrow, shoulder-less road.

11.2 RIGHT on the Norwottuck Rail Trail. You will pass the back of Hampshire Mall, the Amherst Golf Course, the tennis courts of Amherst College, and several hiking trails and conservation areas that invite exploration.

13.2 A tunnel goes under Route 116. For an optional side trip, take the exit just before the tunnel to the Hitchcock Center for the Environment, located about 0.3 mile south on Rte. 116. This nature center provides maps of the 27 Conservation Areas and Trails of Amherst, and is open Wed. through Sat., 9 a.m. to 4 p.m.

15.9 STRAIGHT into the Station Rd. parking area and the end of the ride.

22

Tour of the Hamptons

Rating: Novice to Intermediate
Distance: 25 miles
Terrain: Flat to rolling
Towns: Williamsburg, Northampton, Westhampton, Southampton, Easthampton

Points of Interest: Williamsburg Historical Society, Williamsburg General Store, Westhampton village green, Outlook Farm

Description: Except for two miles on Route 9 this route follows scenic, lightly traveled country roads through the four "Hamptons." This is a pleasant, thoroughly enjoyable ride suitable for all levels of cyclists from novice upward. It is mostly flat but has a few easy hills. Westhampton Center provides a pleasant place to rest, and Outlook Farm and the Williamsburg General Store provide excellent food stops.

Directions:
START from the parking lot behind the Williamsburg Historical Society, near the Williamsburg General Store on Rte. 9 in Williamsburg. (The parking lot entrance is the driveway between the Williamsburg Grange and the Historical Society.)

0.0 RIGHT onto Rte. 9.

1.9 RIGHT onto South Main Street at the Haydenville Library, shortly after The Brass Works. South Main Street bears left, crosses two bridges and becomes River Road at the Northampton Town Line. The route here follows the Mill River.

3.4 STRAIGHT onto Reservoir Rd. and towards the
Reservoir.

3.7 Pass Lower Roberts Meadow Recreation Area and Mayor
David Musante Jr. Beach followed by the Reservoir.

4.8 BEAR RIGHT on Chesterfield Rd. and pass Sylvester
and Kennedy Roads. (You will come out Sylvester and
cross over to Kennedy on the return route).

5.7 BEAR LEFT on Montague Road.

6.0 Westhampton Town Line.

7.1 LEFT onto North Road.

7.8 STRAIGHT to remain on North Rd., which becomes
South Road in Westhampton Center. Ahead on your right
a church spire heralds your approach to Westhampton
Center.

8.8 Benches on the village green provide a pleasant place
to rest. The Congregational Church, the Town Hall, and
the small Westhampton Memorial Library are all set back
from the road. A view of the Mount Tom range can be
seen from the benches. After resting, continue on what is
now South Road, past farms and fields to Rte. 66.

10.1 LEFT onto Rte. 66 and uphill. Hunker down and pedal
up; a reward awaits you at the top, just past the apple
orchard.

10.9 Outlook Farm is much more than a farm stand with fruit
and vegetables; it also has a restaurant, ice cream cones,
home-baked goodies and a very nice restroom. It's a
favorite stop with bicyclists.

10.9 RIGHT on Southampton Rd. Enjoy the beautiful view of
the Mt. Tom range on your left.

12.9 Southampton Town Line.

13.3 RIGHT at the Stop Sign onto Cold Spring Road
(no sign).

14.3 LEFT onto Glendale Rd. (also unmarked). It will
become Torrey Road at the Easthampton Town Line.

15.0 Enjoy a beautiful view of the Mt. Holyoke and Mt. Tom
ranges on your right.

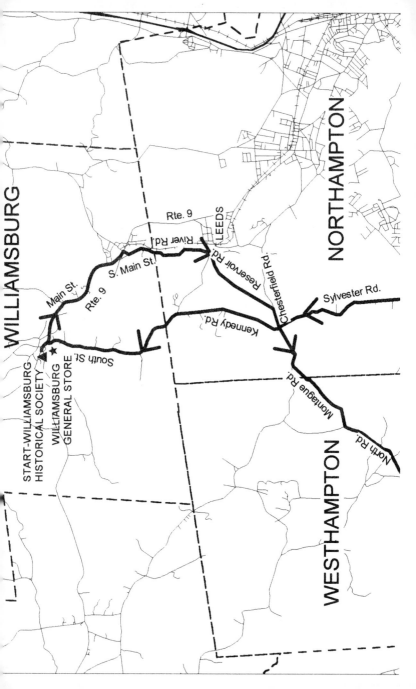

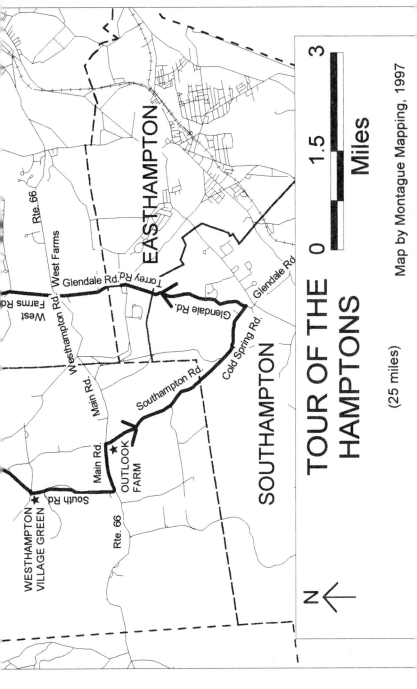

TOUR OF THE HAMPTONS

(25 miles)

Map by Montague Mapping, 1997

Miles

0   1.5   3

N

16.3 STRAIGHT at the Stop Sign and cross Loudville Road
   onto Torrey Road, which will become Glendale Rd. at the
   Northampton Town Line.

17.4 STRAIGHT across Rte. 66 onto West Farms Road.

18.1 STRAIGHT on Sylvester Road in Northampton.
   You will pass Jim's Variety and Package Store.

20.5 CAUTION: Stop, look and listen for fast cars before
   zig-zagging across Chesterfield Road onto Kennedy Rd.

22.2 BEAR LEFT onto South Street (unmarked) at a
   Y intersection.

24.6 LEFT onto Rte. 9 or dismount and take the sidewalk to
   the Williamsburg General Store for ice cream, pastry or
   a cup of coffee.

24.7 LEFT into the driveway between the Williamsburg
   Grange and the Historical Society. End of ride.

23

Up and Over and Down

Rating: Novice, Intermediate, or Advanced
Distance: 15 to 38 miles
Terrain: Hilly
Towns: South Deerfield, Conway, Buckland, Shelburne, Ashfield

Points of Interest: Boyden Brothers' Sugarhouse, Festival of the Hills site, Poverty Pocket Sugarhouse, McCuskers Market, Bridge of Flowers, Glacial Potholes, Salmon Falls Artisans, Baptist Corner Cemetery, Zachary Fields Tavern, Baker's Country Store

Description: The longer version of this ride is not for the faint of heart. It's hilly and there is a stretch of gravel. For the less energetic, there are alternatives which shorten the ride and eliminate some of the hills. Look them over and decide which you want to do. They're all scenic and they're all fun. Three of the rides go to Shelburne Falls, which is a place, not a town. It includes the business districts of Buckland and Shelburne, which are separated by the Deerfield River with a falls and some very impressive glacial potholes. The two towns are connected by the Bridge of Flowers, a former trolley track converted to a footpath bordered with flowers. The rides listed here include one that reverses direction in Conway and another which starts in Conway. Two rides reverse direction in Shelburne Falls. (See Milepoints 7.5 and 16.4 for the options.) Fall is a beautiful time for any of these rides, but they are pretty anytime. A suggestion is to do one of the shorter rides in the spring and one of the longer ones in the fall -- and bring your camera!

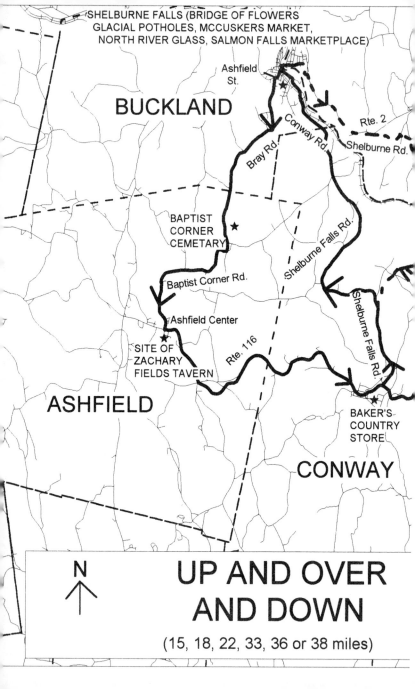

SHELBURNE FALLS (BRIDGE OF FLOWERS
GLACIAL POTHOLES, MCCUSKERS MARKET,
NORTH RIVER GLASS, SALMON FALLS MARKETPLACE)

Ashfield
St.

BUCKLAND

Conway Rd.

Bray Rd.

Rte. 2

Shelburne Rd.

BAPTIST
CORNER
CEMETARY

Shelburne Falls Rd.

Baptist Corner Rd.

Ashfield Center

Shelburne Falls Rd.

SITE OF
ZACHARY
FIELDS TAVERN

Rte. 116

ASHFIELD

BAKER'S
COUNTRY
STORE

CONWAY

N

UP AND OVER
AND DOWN

(15, 18, 22, 33, 36 or 38 miles)

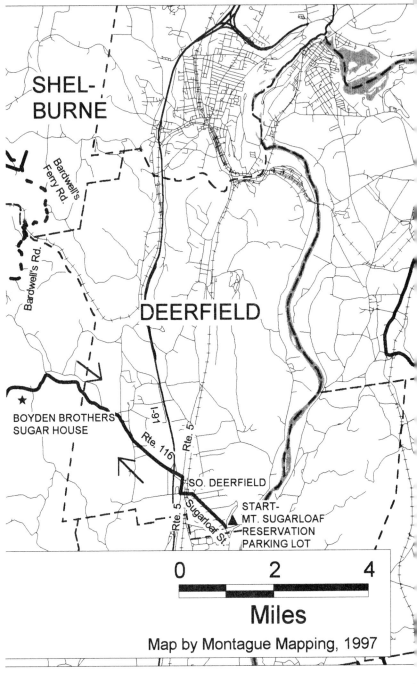

SHEL-
BURNE

Bardwell's Ferry Rd.

Bardwell's Rd.

DEERFIELD

BOYDEN BROTHERS
SUGAR HOUSE

I-91

Rte. 5

Rte. 116

SO. DEERFIELD

Rte. 5

Sugarloaf St.

START-
MT. SUGARLOAF
RESERVATION
PARKING LOT

0   2   4

Miles

Map by Montague Mapping, 1997

Directions:

START at the parking area at the foot of Mt. Sugarloaf
   Reservation on Sugarloaf Street at Rte. 116 in South
   Deerfield.

0.0 RIGHT on Sugarloaf Street, straight through South
   Deerfield to Rte. 5.

1.2 RIGHT on Rte. 5

1.5 LEFT on Rte. 116, which is a long, gradual uphill all
   the way to Conway -- 6 miles.

3.2 Mobil Station and Neighbor's Convenience Store on your
   right has refreshments and restrooms.

6.0 Boyden Brothers Sugarhouse is on your left.

7.2 Pass the Festival of the Hills site, a playing field
   on your left just past Whately Rd. The Festival is
   held every year in late September or early October.

7.5 SHARP RIGHT at the grassy triangle in Conway onto
   scenic Shelburne Falls Rd. You may want to rest on the
   steps of the corner building after the long uphill. At this
   milepoint you have several options:

OPTION A: For a short 15-mile ride, remain on Rte. 116,
   continue 0.2 mile to Baker's Country Store and
   Luncheonette for refreshments and a restroom stop,
   then reverse direction and enjoy the long downhill
   back to the ride start.

OPTION B: START the ride here on Shelburne Falls Rd. and
   bicycle across this scenic ridge to Shelburne
   Falls, reverse direction in Shelburne Falls and
   return to this point for an 18-mile ride.

OPTION C: START here, bicycle to Shelburne Falls,
   continue on the longer route to Ashfield, and return to
   this point for a 22-mile ride.

9.2 LEFT at the fork and uphill towards Shelburne Falls.
   The route becomes flat to rolling, but always scenic,
   before ending on a long downhill into Buckland.

15.6 CAUTION! Railroad tracks at the bottom of the hill! Cross them at a right angle. After the tracks the road will veer right then left, pass the Lamson Knife Factory and enter Buckland along the Deerfield River.

16.4 McCusker's Market on the left is a popular lunch spot with cyclists and the locals. There is a great deli. After lunch, take a sight-seeing walk around Shelburne Falls. Walk over the Bridge of Flowers into Shelburne and down to the Glacial Potholes. On the way, stop at North River Glass and watch the glass blowers. When you have concluded your tour, there are several options for continuing your ride:

OPTION D: Reverse direction and return the way you came for the 18 and 33-mile rides.

OPTION E: For a 36-mile ride, go straight on Bridge St., right on South Maple St., right on Rte. 2, right on Shelburne Rd., sharp right on Bardwell Ferry Rd. at the bottom of a hill, cross the Deerfield River on the Bardwell Ferry Bridge, go uphill (the view at the top is worth it) then down onto Shelburne Falls Rd., and retrace your former route back to Conway, down Rte. 116 and back to the ride start.

OPTION F: Continue onward and upward to Ashfield as follows for the 38-mile ride:

16.4 Go south up Ashfield St. to Salmon Falls Marketplace. Stop and visit, or continue onward and upward.

16.6 RIGHT to stay on Ashfield Street.

16.8 LEFT on Bray Road, a long uphill. Settle down and enjoy the scenery. Its OK to walk. The road goes up in gradual steps with intervals of flatness, ups and downs.

19.7 A mile of hard-packed gravel begins. It will turn to pavement at the historic Baptist Corner Cemetery, then back to gravel just after the cemetery, then pavement for the remainder of the ride.

20.6 STOP at the Cemetery, which will be on your left. Look at the old stones; some date from the 18th century.

20.8 BEAR RIGHT but pause to enjoy the vista on your left before proceeding.

20.9 RIGHT at the stop sign onto Baptist Corner Road. Stay on this road all the way to Rte. 116. Ignore any rights or lefts. Enjoy the beautiful scenery.

23.9 LEFT on Rte. 116 If you look up Rte. 116, the Ashfield Historical Society is on the right. Further up the road but out of sight is the Ashfield General Store (closed Sunday afternoons). Just across the road from where you stand is the former Zachary Field's Tavern (1819-1870). Your route from here is Downhill into Conway! CAUTION: Keep your bike under control.

30.6 Baker's Country Store and Luncheonette on your right has home baked pastry, coffee, ice cream and a restroom.

30.8 PASS your earlier turnoff and retrace your former route downhill. Except for a half-mile stretch past the domed Conway Library, it is down - down - down!

36.8 RIGHT on Rte. 5.

37.2 LEFT at the lights into South Deerfield.

38.3 LEFT into the parking area of the Mount Sugarloaf State Park and, if you haven't had enough hills, there's always the steep climb up to the top of South Sugarloaf Mountain. The view is worth it. However, if you've had enough hills you can always drive up. It's a great place for a picnic.

24

Up the Rail Trail
and Down the Road

Rating: Novice to Intermediate
Distance: 25 miles
Terrain: Flat to rolling
Towns: Northampton, Hadley, Amherst

Points of Interest: Norwottuck Rail Trail, Hadley Town
Common, Salamander Crossing, Cushman Village Store,
North Hadley Sugar Shack, Porter-Phelps-Huntington House

Description: The route begins on the Norwottuck Rail Trail,
named after the Indian tribe that inhabited this area before
the white settlers arrived in the 17th century. This paved trail
follows the former Boston & Maine Railroad right of way
across the Connecticut River, through farmland, woods and
residential areas. The route includes views of Mount Tom,
Mount Holyoke Range, Mount Toby and Mount Sugarloaf.
The trail crosses the Hadley Common and passes through
several conservation areas in Amherst. This is a thoroughly
delightful rail trail, but heavily used, so cyclists should be on
the alert for skaters, walkers, children and baby strollers. The
return trip is via scenic country roads, passing horse farms,
tobacco barns, strawberry fields, corn fields, sugar shack, and
historic houses. The Cushman Village Store provides an
opportunity for refreshments and the Cushman Village
Common provides a place to relax. Mountain and river views
enhance the scenery. The route returns to the Rail Trail to
cross the river at the end of the trip. For further information
about the Rail Trail, consult *Great Rail-Trails of the
Northeast* (see listing in References, page 167).

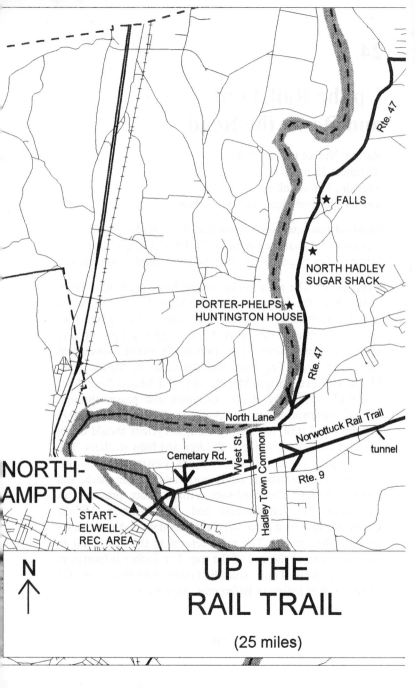

FALLS

NORTH HADLEY
SUGAR SHACK

PORTER-PHELPS
HUNTINGTON HOUSE

Rte. 47

Rte. 47

North Lane

Norwottuck Rail Trail

tunnel

Cemetary Rd.

West St.

Hadley Town Common

Rte. 9

NORTH-
AMPTON

START-
ELWELL
REC. AREA

N

UP THE
RAIL TRAIL

(25 miles)

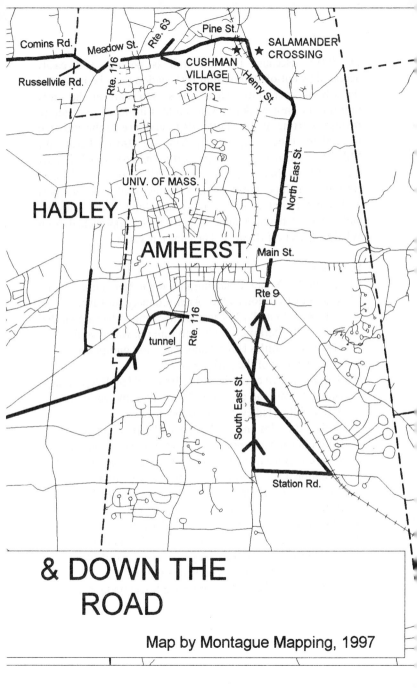

Comins Rd.

Russellvile Rd.

Meadow St.

Rte. 116

Rte. 63

Pine St.

CUSHMAN
VILLAGE
STORE

SALAMANDER
CROSSING

Henry St.

North East St.

UNIV. OF MASS.

HADLEY

AMHERST

Main St.

Rte 9

tunnel

Rte. 116

South East St.

Station Rd.

& DOWN THE
ROAD

Map by Montague Mapping, 1997

OPTIONS: Because the rail trail is popular and easily accessed by out-of-staters from I-91, parking can be limited at the Elwell Recreation Area. Unless you start in the early morning or on a weekday, you might want to do this ride in reverse, starting at the Station Road entrance to the rail trail in Amherst (See milepost 9.0). You can also start from the Mill River Recreation Area in North Amherst, which is only 0.3 mile from Pine Street at Route 63 (See milepost 16.4), or start from behind the Mountain Farms Mall (See milepost 4.1). Another option is to start from behind Valley Bicycles and the Ice Cream Pedaler, which can be approached from Whalley Street off Route 9. The choice is yours.

Directions:

START at the Damon Road entrance to the Norwottuck Rail Trail in Elwell Recreation Area, Connecticut River Greenway State Park. Clean composting toilets are on the right of the parking area but no running water, so fill your water bottles beforehand. The Trail entrance is at the left end of the parking area.

0.0 CROSS the river on the old railroad bridge. Keep to the right, stop at road crossings. Ride safely and courteously.

1.7 CROSS the Hadley Town Common.

2.0 Valley Bicycles and the Ice Cream Pedaler on your right offer repairs, rentals, and refreshments. They may also be approached from Whalley Street off Route 9 for an optional ride start (see milepost 23.7 below).

3.3 Make a noise before entering the tunnel under Route 9. Ring your bell, blow your horn, or holler!

3.4 Hungry or thirsty? Stop at Pete's Drive-In.

4.1 Bread and Circus at Mountain Farms Mall offers a natural food stop and parking area for optional start.

5.2 Amherst Golf Course is on your right.

5.7 CROSS over the bridge with Snell Street underneath.

6.2 Another tunnel! This one goes under Route 116. You can take the exit here for a short side trip to the Hitchcock Center for the Environment, located about 0.5 mile south on Rte. 116. This nature center provides maps of the 27 Conservation Areas and Trails of Amherst, as well as information about salamanders (See milepost 15.0 below). The Center is open Wed. through Sat., 9 a.m. to 4 p.m.

7.9 Poor Farms Swamp is on your left.

9.0 Leave the bike path through the parking lot; go RIGHT onto Station Rd. This is a gentle uphill past woods, the Lawrence Swamp Conservation Area, Hop Brook, the Robert Frost Hiking Trail, and two horse farms.

9.9 RIGHT on Southeast Street, a slightly hilly and scenic stretch of farmland with views of the Pelham hills to your right.

12.0 CROSS Route 9 at the lights.

12.3 CROSS Main St. at another set of lights onto Northeast Street. Gentle hills, farmland and views of the Pelham hills continue. Northeast Street becomes Henry Street.

15.0 Salamander Crossing! Miniature fences on each side of the road provide access to tunnels for salamanders which migrate every spring to breed at a pond on the downhill side of the road. You won't see them; they migrate at night during the first heavy spring rain.

15.1 LEFT on Pine St. Cross the R.R. tracks carefully. Stop at the Cushman Village Store for refreshments. Relax on the Village Common across from the store.

16.4 CROSS Rte. 63 at the lights in North Amherst onto Meadow Street.

16.7 CROSS Rte. 116 at the lights and continue on Meadow Street.

16.9 RIGHT on Russellville Road through more farmland.

18.3 LEFT on Rte. 47 in North Hadley. Farmland will continue. The Mount Holyoke range will come into view on your left and the Connecticut River will be on your right.

20.3 In North Hadley Center, pass Lake Warner on your left and stop to observe the falls flowing over a dam at the site of the first corn mill in the area. Take time to read the plaque on the boulder for some interesting information.

20.8 The North Hadley Sugar Shack on your left pours forth steam from boiling sap in the spring. Sugar buckets hang on maple trees up and down Route 47 at that time.

21.6 The historic Porter-Phelps-Huntington House on your right holds concerts and teas during the summer and is open to the public for tours.

23.0 RIGHT on North Lane and along the dike that prevents the Connecticut River from overflowing its banks in the springtime after heavy rains.

23.4 LEFT onto West St. on the further side of the Common, but first you may want to stop for a view of the River from the dike.

23.7 RIGHT on Cemetery Road past a cemetery, tree farm and more farmland. (If you started the ride at Valley Bicycles, continue on West Street and take a LEFT onto the Rail Trail.)

24.5 SHARP LEFT on a blind turn at the top of the rise. CAUTION: Keep far right to avoid possible oncoming cars!

25.3 RIGHT onto the Norwottuck Rail Trail and over the converted railroad bridge.

25.4 End of ride.

25

Up the River
and Over to Old Deerfield

Rating: Novice
Distance: 21 miles
Terrain: Flat to rolling
Towns: Sunderland, Deerfield

Points of Interest: Sunderland's Main Street, Connecticut River, Old Deerfield, Deerfield River, Bloody Brook, Captain Lathrop Monument

Description: This ride follows the Connecticut and Deerfield Rivers to the historic village of Old Deerfield. Attacked and nearly destroyed during the French and Indian War, this former frontier outpost is now a handsome and prosperous village. Twelve historic homes are open to the public; guided tours are available. Plan to spend some time exploring Old Deerfield but also enjoy the route to and from the village. The ride starts in Sunderland, travels past stately 18th and 19th century residences, turns onto Route 116, crosses the Connecticut River, then turns onto River Road and follows the river upstream. In South Deerfield you will encounter another bit of history at the site of the Battle of Bloody Brook. On the home stretch you will enjoy views of the Pocumtuck Range, Mount Sugarloaf and Mount Toby before crossing the Connecticut River again and completing this scenic and historic ride. The route can be shortened by starting on River Road or the base of Mount Sugarloaf (See the OPTIONS in directions below).

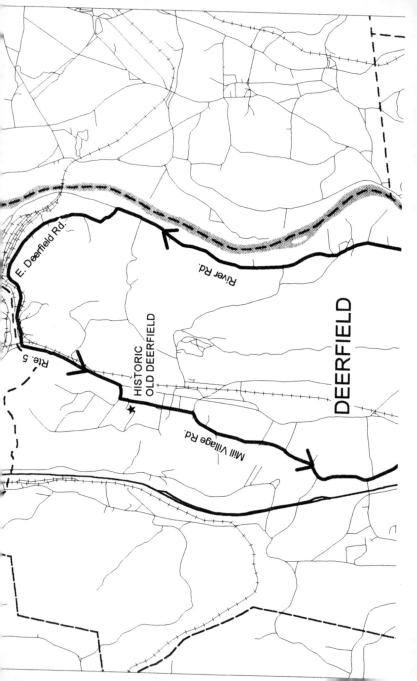

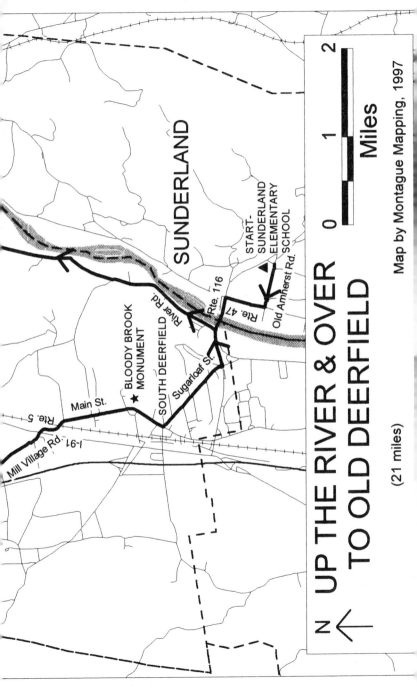

UP THE RIVER & OVER
TO OLD DEERFIELD

(21 miles)

Map by Montague Mapping, 1997

N

SUNDERLAND

START-
SUNDERLAND
ELEMENTARY
SCHOOL

Old Amherst Rd.

Rte. 47

Rte. 116

River Rd.

BLOODY BROOK
MONUMENT

SOUTH DEERFIELD

Sugarloaf St.

Main St.

Rte. 5

Mill Village Rd.

I-91

Miles

0   1   2

Directions:

START at the Sunderland Elementary School on Swampfield Drive off Old Amherst Road, which is off Route 116 in Sunderland.

0.2 RIGHT onto Old Amherst Road.

0.6 RIGHT on Route 47, Sunderland's attractive Main St.

1.0 LEFT at the lights onto Route 116 and cross the bridge over the Connecticut River.

1.4 RIGHT on River Road on the other side of the bridge and go along the river. This scenic road is popular with bicyclists. There are a few gentle hills but they are matched by lovely views and good downhills.

8.1 BEAR LEFT and up a short hill to continue on River Road. Leave the Connecticut river behind and pick up the Deerfield River near the end of River Road.

10.8 LEFT on Route 5. Pass the Wok Restaurant and a few antique shops. Watch for the Historic Deerfield sign on your right.

12.1 RIGHT on Old Deerfield Street after the above sign.

12.3 LEFT at the Y-intersection into the village. Ride slowly or walk to fully appreciate its uniqueness.

12.4 The Indian House and the Channing Blake Meadow Walk are on your right. Visit the gift shop in back of the Indian House. Take the short, pleasant meadow walk.

12.6 The Deerfield Inn and the Museum Store are on your right. A cafeteria with a patio in back of the Inn is a pleasant place to stop for refreshments. The Historic Deerfield Information Center is across from the Inn. There are picnic tables and public restrooms in back of the Information Center.

12.8 Memorial Street on your left leads to the Memorial Hall Museum. This street is closed off for the very popular Deerfield Crafts Fair for one weekend each spring and fall. The Museum has a gift shop and rest rooms as well as interesting exhibits.

13.1   RIGHT on Mill Village Road at the Y through farmland and along the Deerfield River. The Pocumtuck Range will be on your left until the road curves left and brings you out to Route 5.

16.6   CROSS Route 5 to Main Street in South Deerfield. (A side trip to the right on Route 5 will take you to the Yankee Candle Factory).

17.7   Bloody Brook: A monument in the small park on your left memorializes Captain Thomas Lathrop, who was slain with 76 of his men at the Battle of Bloody Brook. This small brook flows under the road and might not be noticed except for a sign on the right.

18.3   LEFT on Sugarloaf Street at the town center. There are numerous eating places in the vicinity if you are hungry or thirsty.

19.3   LEFT on Route 116 just past the entrance to Mount Sugarloaf State Park. Cross the bridge over the Connecticut River into Sunderland.

20.2   RIGHT on Route 47 at the Congregational Church.

20.7   LEFT on Old Amherst Road.

21.0   LEFT on Swampfield Street into the Elementary School parking lot and end of the ride.

26

Water, Water Everywhere

Rating: Intermediate
Distance: 33 miles
Terrain: Flat to hilly
Towns: Amherst, Leverett, Shutesbury, Montague,
Sunderland, Hadley

Points of Interest: The falls at Puffer's Pond, Cushman
Brook, Sawmill River, Lake Wyola, Village Co-op, Montague
Mill, the falls on Falls Road in Sunderland

Description: This ride follows several streams and passes by
several lakes or ponds, as well as three waterfalls. It has one
long uphill and several long downhills plus a long flat stretch.
It's a pretty ride, passing through farmland and rural areas,
and there are two great food stops.

Directions:
START at the Mill River Recreation Area off Rte. 63 in
   North Amherst center.
0.0 RIGHT on Rte. 63 from the Recreation Area.
0.1 RIGHT on Summer Street.
0.5 RIGHT on Mill Street and across the Mill River.
   Observe the falls coming over Puffer's Pond dam on your
   left. Caution! Narrow bridge, narrow road, blind curve
   and short steep pitch to State Street.
0.6 LEFT on State Street. Puffer's Pond, as it is locally
   known, is on your left. Its official name is Factory
   Hollow Pond. Swimming is permitted and there is a
   portable toilet but no lifeguard. This is a very popular
   spot and it can be crowded in the summer.

0.8 Cushman Brook flows into the pond and will be on your right as you bicycle up State Street. There is a swimming hole on the right at the end of the street that can be accessed by crossing a grassy plot and walking down the bank. Its O.K. to swim there.

1.3 LEFT on East Leverett Road. Cushman Brook will continue on your right. This is a pretty stretch of road with woods, farmland and a few houses. East Leverett Road will become Cushman Road in Leverett.

3.3 LEFT on Cushman Road and across Roaring Brook.

3.5 RIGHT on Shutesbury Road, a long gradual uphill. Roaring Brook will continue on your right, then left, then right as you cycle along. This road is especially beautiful in June when the mountain laurel is in bloom.

5.5 Shutesbury Road becomes Leverett Road in Shutesbury.

7.6 LEFT onto Wendell Road. You've reached the top! Stop for a well-deserved rest on Shutesbury Common. When you continue, you will be on a sparsely settled ridge.

9.8 LEAVE Wendell Road which becomes gravel and goes off to your right. GO STRAIGHT on Locks Pond Road. A long downhill follows -- enjoy it!

11.1 Randall Road on your right leads to the Shutesbury Conservation Area public beach on Lake Wyola. It's a delightful spot for a swim and it's free. The main beach is state-owned and there is a fee.

11.7 LEFT on Lakeview/North Leverett Road. Lake Wyola is on your right. Sawmill River flows out of Lake Wyola and will be on your left as you bicycle downhill to Moore's Corner in Leverett and a stop at the Village Co-op.

13.6 LEFT on Rattlesnake Gutter Road and RIGHT into the Village Co-op, a great place to take a break. It has rest rooms, hot and cold food and beverages, a porch, and picnic tables under the trees. After taking your break, return to North Leverett Road and enjoy more downhill as you head towards Montague. The Sawmill River reappears on your right.

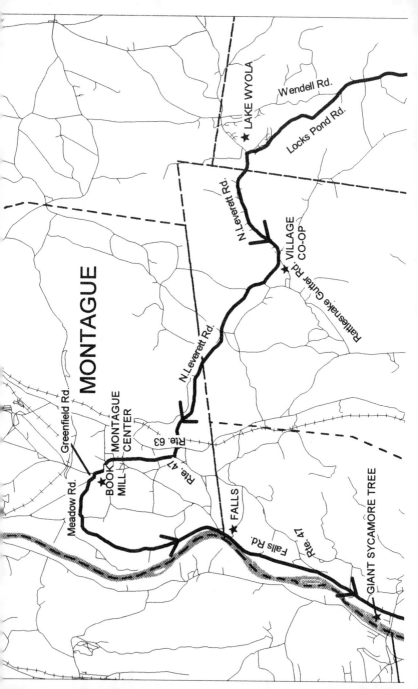

MONTAGUE

LAKE WYOLA

Wendell Rd.

Locks Pond Rd.

N. Leverett Rd.

VILLAGE CO-OP

Rattlesnake Gutter Rd.

N. Leverett Rd.

Greenfield Rd.

MONTAGUE CENTER

BOOK MILL

Meadow Rd.

Rte. 63

Rte. 41

FALLS

Falls Rd.

Rte. 47

GIANT SYCAMORE TREE

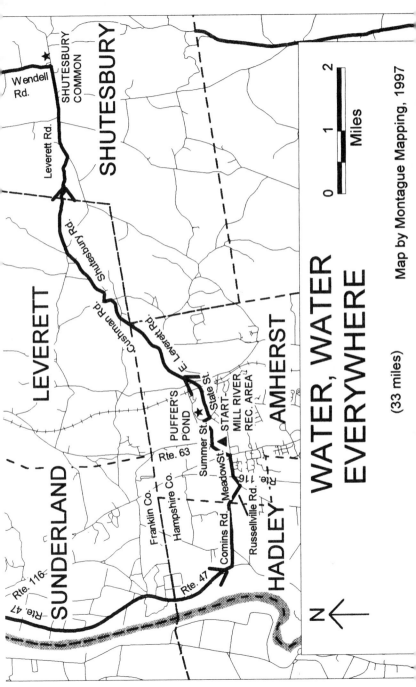

WATER, WATER
EVERYWHERE

(33 miles)

Map by Montague Mapping, 1997

15.4 Observe the sawmill and adjacent dam and waterfall on your left. It operated as a water-powered sawmill into the 1990s.

17.5 CROSS Rte. 63. Follow the Sawmill River, now on your right, into Montague Center.

18.8 BEAR LEFT at the Common.

19.0 Bear RIGHT towards Turners Falls. Cross the bridge over the Sawmill River. The Montague Mill will be visible on your left.

19.1 LEFT on Greenfield Road and down the driveway to the Montague Mill and Blue Heron Cafe. A restroom is available in the Montague Mill. Enjoy the view of the water from the Cafe or the outside deck.

19.2 LEFT on Greenfield Rd. from the Montague Mill.

19.3 LEFT on Meadow Rd. and stay left when it intersects North Ferry Road. This scenic road is popular with bicyclists. Expect to see a few. Meadow Road will become Falls Road in Sunderland.

22.8 Observe the falls for which the road is named. The falls are on your left; the Connecticut River is on your right.

24.5 RIGHT on Rte. 47, Sunderland's tree-lined Main Street.

24.8 Observe the giant sycamore. It was there 200 years ago when the constitution was signed, as is explained by the monument in front of the tree.

26.0 CROSS Rte. 116 in Sunderland center and continue on Rte. 47 all the way to North Hadley. The Dairy Mart on the corner of 116 on your right has a restroom as well as refreshments. The Millstone Farm Market just down the street on the left also has refreshments. A long, flat stretch of scenic farmland decorated with tobacco sheds follows. A farm on the left sells ice cream, fruit, and vegestables.

29.2 LEFT on Comins Road, which becomes Russellville Road in Amherst and includes more farms and a view of the University of Massachusetts.

31.6 LEFT at the T-intersection onto Meadow Street. Cross Eastman Brook, followed by the Mill River.

31.7 Cross Rte. 116 at the lights and continue on Meadow Street to the next set of lights.

32.1 LEFT at the lights onto Rte. 63. Pass the Riverside Park shops and cross the Mill River again.

32.4 RIGHT into the Mill River Recreation Area. If you haven't had enough water, you may want to take a swim in the pool behind the building, go wading in the river, or return to Puffer's Pond for a swim.

27

Way to Wendell

Rating: Intermediate
Distance: 22 to 36 miles
Terrain: Flat to hilly
Towns: Leverett, Shutesbury, Wendell, Montague

Points of Interest: Village Co-op in Moores' Corner, Lake Wyola, Wendell Country Store, Wendell State Forest, Ruggles Pond, Hunting Hills Store, old sawmill and falls in the village of North Leverett

Description: This popular route starts from the Village Co-op in Moores' Corner in Leverett, providing refreshments and a restroom at the beginning and end of the ride. It follows the Sawmill River from Leverett to Lake Wyola State Park in Shutesbury, then turns north to Wendell. The road to Wendell is wooded and rural and there are ponds on both sides of the road. At the ponds there is an optional shortcut over to Wendell State Forest. The main route, however, continues into Wendell Center, turns downhill at the Common, and passes Wendell State Forest, which offers swimming, hiking, mountain biking, and (in winter) cross-country skiing. The route continues downhill to Route 63, which is relatively flat. Hunting Hills on Route 63 offers another food stop, and North Leverett Road brings you back to the Village Co-op. This ride is hilly, but none of the hills are steep, and the downhills are rewarding. This is a popular ride with cyclists who know it.

Directions:
START from the Village Co-op at the intersection of North Leverett Road and Rattlesnake Gutter Road in the village of Moores Corner, town of Leverett.

0.0 LEFT out of the parking lot onto Rattlesnake Gutter Road and right on North Leverett Rd. The Sawmill River tumbles down on your right as you bicycle uphill.

2.0 PASS Locks Pond Road and the outlet of Lake Wyola on your right.

2.1 PASS Lake Wyola State Park; the lake is on your right.

2.7 LEFT on Locks Village Rd. past the Pine Brook Camp and Retreat Center (Camp Anderson), a church camp, heading towards Wendell Depot.

4.8 PASS Lock Hill Rd. on your right and STAY on Locks Village Rd. (*OPTION:* For a shortcut, skip Wendell center and take West Street ahead on the left, to Montague Rd to Wendell State Forest and out to Rte. 63.) The main route continues into Wendell center.

5.6 STOP at the Wendell Country Store and Red's Cafe for refreshments and a restroom.

6.1 LEFT on Montague Rd. opposite the Common and downhill to Wendell State Forest.

9.8 RIGHT at Forest Headquarters to Ruggles Pond to swim, picnic, relax, use the comfort station, or just enjoy the scenery. Then return to Montague Road.

10.3 RIGHT on Montague Road and continue downhill with CAUTION! The road becomes curving as it approaches Route 63. Maintain control of your bicycle.

13.4 BEAR LEFT; do not cross the bridge.

13.8 LEFT on Rte. 63, which will be flat.

17.2 Hunting Hills offers another food stop.

18.0 LEFT on North Leverett Rd. towards Lake Wyola State Park.

20.1 Village of North Leverett: Stop at the former sawmill and view the falls.

21.8 RIGHT on Rattlesnake Gutter Road and right into the parking lot at the Village Co-op. End of the ride and another chance for refreshments and restrooms.

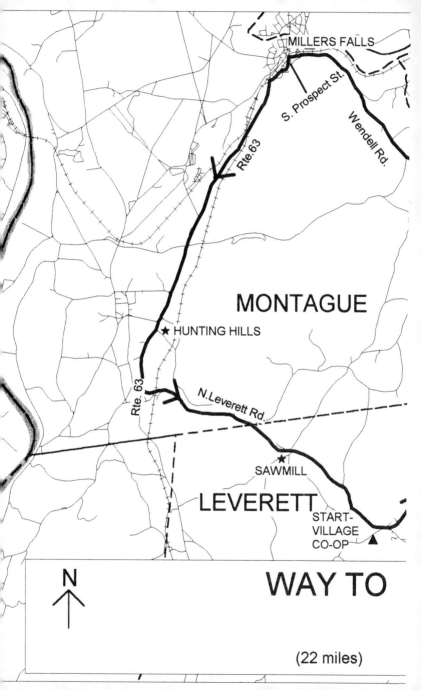

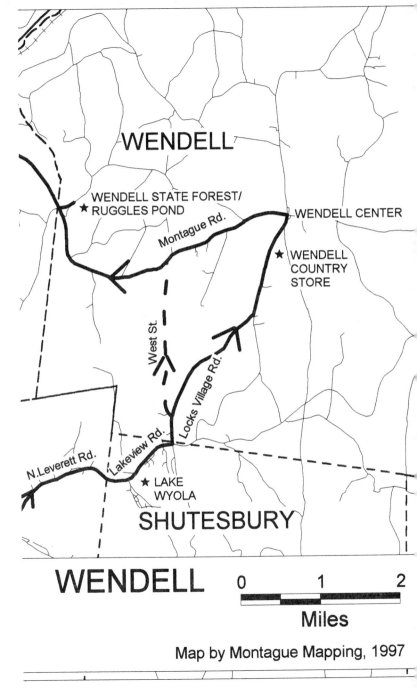

WENDELL

WENDELL STATE FOREST/
★ RUGGLES POND

WENDELL CENTER

Montague Rd.

★ WENDELL
COUNTRY
STORE

West St.

Locks Village Rd.

N. Leverett Rd.

Lakeview Rd.

★ LAKE
WYOLA

SHUTESBURY

WENDELL

0   1   2

Miles

Map by Montague Mapping, 1997

28

West Pelham Hills

Rating: Intermediate to Advanced
Distance: 17 miles
Terrain: Hilly
Towns: Amherst, Pelham, Shutesbury, Leverett

Points of Interest: Amethyst Brook Conservation Area, Metacomet-Monadnock Trail, Atkins Reservoir, Cushman Village Store, Salamander Crossing

Description: As the title suggests, this ride is hilly. However, the beauty of the surroundings and the long downhill more than compensate for the uphill. A shortcut on a downhill gravel road can eliminate some of the hilliness, but sturdy touring tires are advisable for this option. The route in general is lightly traveled, sparsely populated, and scenic. It is easier to ride in the fall than in the spring, due to road conditions. The ride described here starts from the Fort River School on Southeast Street in Amherst, but you can also start from Amethyst Brook Conservation Area on Pelham Road. Because the route traces a loop, you can also start it from wherever you choose, or ride the following directions in reverse.

Directions:
START from the Fort River School on Southeast St. between
    Rte. 9 and Main St. in Amherst.
0.0 RIGHT out of the Fort River School driveway onto
    Southeast Street.
0.1 RIGHT onto Main St./Pelham Rd. and begin a gradual
    uphill.

0.7 PASS Amethyst Brook Conservation Area on your left.

1.7 LEFT on North Valley Road, which starts out flat (a welcome respite), followed by a short downhill before starting to climb where the road crosses Amethyst Brook. Buffum Brook, which flows into Amethyst Brook, tumbles down on the right.

2.3 The parking area for the Metacomet-Monadnock Hiking Trail is on your left. If you hike south on this trail, you'll end up in Connecticut. If you hike north, you'll end up in New Hampshire. The trail goes into the woods on your right at a double blaze. Keep to the road.

2.9 LEFT on Buffum Road. There is a long stretch of woods, rolling hills, and an occasional home.

4.9 Entering Shutesbury. Buffum Rd. becomes West Pelham Road. The area becomes more populated but still woodsy.

5.7 Sandhill Road on your left. *OPTION:* Taking this road shortens the ride, but use caution. It is gravel and downhill. If you choose this shortened route, watch for these turns:

> LEFT on Pratts Corner Rd.
> RIGHT on Cross Rd. to Cushman Rd.
> LEFT on Cushman Rd. Pass Atkins Reservoir. (No swimming; this is an Amherst water supply.)
> LEFT on Market Hill Rd.
> LEFT on Henry St. Watch for salamander crossings.
> STRAIGHT on Northeast St.
> CROSS Main St.
> LEFT into Fort River School driveway.

5.7 STRAIGHT on West Pelham Rd. to continue the longer ride.

7.8 LEFT on Leverett/Shutesbury Rd. and reap your reward, a long, beautiful, curved downhill! CAUTION! Maintain control of your bike!

11.1 LEFT on Cushman Road and cross the bridge over Roaring Brook, which has accompanied you downhill.

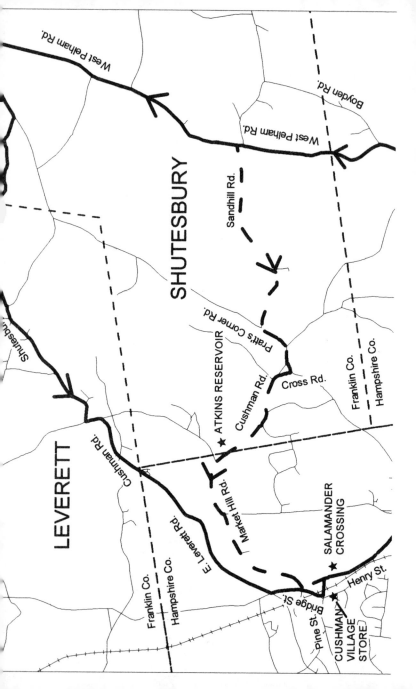

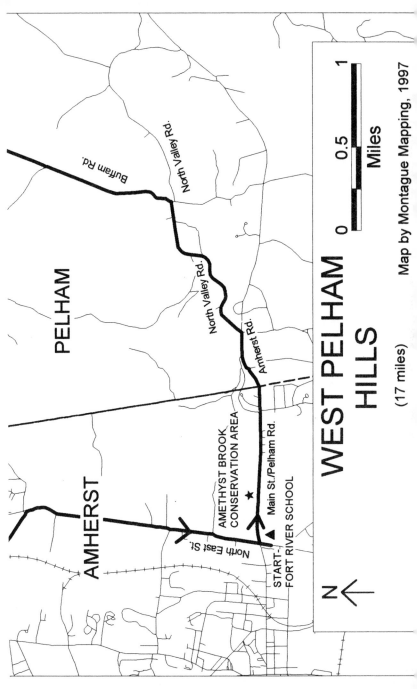

PELHAM

AMHERST

Buffam Rd.

North Valley Rd.

North Valley Rd.

Amherst Rd.

AMETHYST BROOK
CONSERVATION AREA

North East St.

Main St./Pelham Rd.

START-
FORT RIVER SCHOOL

WEST PELHAM
HILLS

(17 miles)

N

Miles

0   0.5   1

Map by Montague Mapping, 1997

11.2 RIGHT and continue on Cushman Rd., which becomes East Leverett Rd. in Amherst. Watch for the Scottish cattle on your right. They're pretty impressive.

13.5 CAUTION: angled railroad tracks. Cross at an angle to avoid ensnaring your wheels.

13.6 LEFT at the Cushman Village Common to the Cushman Village Store on Pine St. for refreshments. Then take a well-deserved rest on the Common.

13.6 LEFT on Pine St. from the Common or RIGHT from the Store and cross the R.R. tracks.

13.7 RIGHT on Henry St. Go slowly. Salamander crossing.

13.8 First tunnel; a second follows. Observe the tunnels under the road and the little fences to the side that guide the salamanders into the tunnels. The tunnels were built by the town of Amherst to facilitate the salamanders migrating to the pond on the opposite side of the street each spring to reproduce. Before the tunnels were built, many salamanders were squashed by cars, despite attempts by nature lovers to handcarry them.

14.6 STRAIGHT onto Northeast St. Observe the Pelham Hills up there on your left, hills that you just biked.

16.5 CROSS Main St. at the lights.

16.7 Second LEFT into the Fort River School parking area; the first left is an exit only. End of the ride.

References

Adventure Cycling Association. *Cyclosource.* Adventure Cycling, P.O. Box 8308, Missoula, MO 59807 -- Catalog of maps, books and gear for the adventure cyclist.

Adventure Cycling Association. *The Cyclists Yellow Pages.* Adventure Cycling, Missoula, MO 59807 -- A soft-cover directory for bicycle trip planning issued annually by ACA: maps, books, routes and rides.

Anybody's Bike Book - 20th Anniversary Edition. Ten Speed Press, P.O.Box 7123, Berkeley, CA 94797 -- Time-tested maintenance and repair tips.

Bicycling Magazine's Complete Guide to Bicycle Repair and Maintenance. St. Martin's Press, 175 5th Ave., N.Y., N.Y.

Conuel, Thomas. *Quabbin: The Accidental Wilderness.* Mass. Audubon Society, Lincoln, MA -- The history and ecology of the Quabbin Reservoir.

Cuthbertson, Tom and Rick Morall. *The Bike Bag Book.* Ten Speed Press, Berkeley, CA 94797 -- A manual for emergency roadside repairs.

Della Pella, Craig. *Great Rail-Trails of the Northeast.* New England Cartographics, P.O. Box 9369, North Amherst MA 01059. Detailed information on the Norwottuck Rail Trail, Northampton Bike Path, and the Rails-to-Trails Conservancy.

Editors of Bicycling Magazine. *New Bike Owner's Guide.* Rodale Press, Emmaus, PA -- How to buy, maintain and repair your bicycle.

Farny, Michael H. *New England Over the Handlebars.* Little Brown and Company, Boston -- Touring book, which includes coastal tours, river tours, and mountain tours. Three of the tours are in the Connecticut River Valley.

Forester, John. *Effective Cycling*. The MIT Press, Mass. Institute of Technology, Cambridge MA 02142. -- Detailed book on proper riding techniques with emphasis on safety.

Jane, Nancy. *Bicycle Touring in the Pioneer Valley*. The University of Mass. Press., Amherst MA 01003. 16 tours in the Pioneer Valley with variations.

Metacomet-Monadnock Trail Guide. Berkshire Chapter, Appalachian Mountain Club, P.O. Box 9369, North Amherst, MA 01059

Nye, Peter. *The Cyclist's Sourcebook*. The Putnam Publishing Group, East Rutherford, NJ -- A guide to equipment, services, tours and other bicycling information.

Thomas, Paul. *The Best Bike Rides in New England.* Globe Pequot Press, Old Saybrook, CT 06475. Includes one 55-mile ride in the Pioneer Valley.

Tobey, Eric and Richard Wolkenberg. *Northeast Bicycle Tours*. Tobey Publishing Co., Inc., New Canaan, CT 06840. --130 tours in New York and New England. Includes four tours in the Pioneer Valley.

Touring Jacob's Ladder by Bicycle and Car. Pioneer Valley Planning Commission, 26 Central St., West Springfield MA 01089

Van der Plas, Rob. *Roadside Bicycle Repairs*. Bicycle Books, P.O. Box 2038, Mill Valley, CA 94941 -- Simple, systematic and inexpensive.

Van der Plas, Rob. *The Bicycle Touring Manual*. Bicycle Books, P.O. Box 2038, Mill Valley, CA 94942 -- A complete source for all information related to bicycles and touring.

Maps

Bicycle Map of Connecticut. Conn. Dept. of Transportation, P.O. Drawer A, Engineering Records, 24 Wolcott Hill Rd., Wethersfield, CT 06109

Guide to Amherst Conservation Areas and Trails. The Kestrel Trust. PO Box 1016, Amherst MA 01004. $3.00. This guide and individual Amherst Conservation Area maps are also available at the Hitchcock Center for the Environment, 525 South Pleasant St., Amherst MA 01002.

Hampshire County Road & Street Map. Arrow Map, Inc., 25 Constitution Drive, Taunton MA 02780

JIMAPCO Western Massachusetts Road Maps for: *Franklin County, Hampshire County, Berkshire County, Hampden County,* and *Greater Springfield, Massachusetts.* Available in many convenience stores for $3.00 to $4.00.

A Map of Hampshire County. The D.H.Jones Real Estate Group, 200 Triangle St., Amherst MA 01002

Massachusetts Bicycle Map. Mass. Dept. of Public Works and the Metropolitan Area Planning Council, Boston, MA

Pioneer Valley Bicycling Guide. Lower Pioneer Valley Regional Planning Commission. 26 Central St., West Springfield, MA 01089

Quabbin Reservation Guide. New England Cartographics, P.O. Box 9369, North Amherst, MA 01059. $4.95 postpaid.

Western Mass Bicycle and Road Map, Rubel Bike Maps, PO Box 1035, Cambridge MA 02140. $5.25 postpaid. Highly recommended. Available at local bike shops.

Bicycling Organizations

League of American Bicyclists
1612 "K" St. N.W., Suite 401, Washington DC 20006
Tel. (202) 822-1333   Fax (202) 822-1334

The *League of American Bicyclists* was founded in 1880 as the League of American Wheelmen. It protects the rights and promotes the interests of bicyclists, provides information about bicycling for members and others, serves a nationwide network of affiliated bicycle clubs and advocacy organizations, and sponsors bicycle rallies, including Pedaling for Power charity rides. *Bicycle USA* is published 6 times a year.

Adventure Cycling Organization
P.O. Box 8308, Missoula, MT 59807-8308

The *Adventure Cycling Organization* is a nonprofit service organization for recreational touring bicyclists. Since its incorporation in 1974 as Bikecentennial, *Adventure Cycling* has developed and mapped a nationwide network of bicycle touring routes and has produced a variety of publications and services for bicyclists, including *The Cyclists Yellow Pages*, a complete trip planning resource; the *Cyclosource Catalog*, a collection of books, maps, and specialty products; and a Tours Program that offers a wide variety of organized tours ranging from 7 to 93 days in length. Its publication *Adventure Cycling* is published 9 times a year.

Tandem Club of America
2220 Vanessa Drive, Birmingham, AL 35242-4430

The *Tandem Club of America* is a volunteer-operated club consisting of tandem cyclists who sponsor rides and rallies across the U.S. The Eastern Tandem Rally is held annually in New England; the 1990 rally was held at UMASS Amherst. The newsletter *Doubletalk* is published 6 times a year.

Rails-to-Trails Conservancy
1100 17th St. NW, 10th floor, Washington, D.C. 20036

The vision of the *Rails-to-Trails Conservancy* is to preserve abandoned railroad corridors and create a nationwide network of trails for public use, connecting cities with countryside, and linking communities to both workplaces and recreation.

Mass Bike
214A Broadway, Cambridge MA 02139

Formerly known as the Bicycle Coalition of Massachusetts, *Mass Bike* advocates for pro-bicycle legislation, promotes bikeway development, supports bicycle safety programs, and offers a wide range of community bicycling events.

Local Bicycling Clubs

The following local bicycle clubs sponsor weekly rides (in season) and other activities such as potlucks, meetings, and banquets. They also publish newsletters and ride schedules. Membership is open to the public and fees are reasonable.

Cyclonauts Bicycling Club
  Les Prentice, Treasurer
  1472 Plumtree Road, Springfield, MA 01119

The Cyclonauts ride mainly in the Springfield area. Off season, they schedule hikes and cross-country skiing.

Franklin-Hampshire Freewheelers
  Al Shane, Treasurer
  20 Two Mile Road, Amherst, MA 01002

The Freewheelers ride mainly in Hampshire and Franklin counties.

Bicycle Stores
413 Area Code

Action Sports & Bikes
    390 East St., Ludlow   **547-2628**
Aggressive Tread
    94 Thompson St., Springfield   **734-3678**
Apollo Bicycle Center,
    23 Hamburg St., Springfield   **781-3019**
Axler's Bicycle Corner
    313 Springfield St., Agawam   **786-4994**
    16 Armory St., Northampton   **585-1188**
Basically Bicycles
    88 Third St., Turners Falls   **863-3556**
Bianco & Sons Bicycle Center
    1110 Springfield. St., Feeding Hills   **786-8660**
Bicycle Barn
    56 Main St., Northfield   **498-2996**
Bicycle Dynamics
    15 College Hwy., Southampton   **529-2537**
Bicycle World
    63 South Pleasant St., Amherst   **253-7722**
    104 Federal St., Greenfield   **774-3701**
    32A Masonic St., Northampton   **585-9100**
Bicycles Unlimited
    322 High St., Greenfield   **772-2700**
Bob's Bike Shop
    15 Vreeland Av., E. Longmeadow   **734-6843**
Competitive Edge Ski & Bike
    Route 9, Hadley   **585-8833**
    Route 5, Holyoke   **538-7662**
Country Bike & Sports
    12 Exchange St., Barre   **(978) 355-2219**
Custom Cycle
    88 Elm St., Westfield   **568-6036**

Easthampton Bicycle
    57 Union St., Easthampton   **529-0319**

Family Bike & Sports
    217-L Shaker Rd., E. Longmeadow   **525-2346**

F. J. Rogers Co.
    3 Main St., Florence   **584-1727**

Highland Hardware & Bike Shop
    917 Hampden, Holyoke   **539-9314**

Mickey's Bike Shop
    520 East St., Chicopee   **592-4282**

New Horizon Sports, Inc.
    55 Franklin St., Westfield   **562-5237**

Northampton Bicycle
    319 Pleasant St., Northampton   **586-3810**

Peak Performance Bicycle Shop
    1584 Dwight, Holyoke   **535-2453**

Pro Bicycle Shop
    1344 Allen St., Springfield   **783-4834**

Rob's Precision Bicycle
    16-C North Maple St., Florence   **585-5930**

Ski-In (Wheels in Motion)
    2006 Boston Rd., Wilbraham   **543-4980**
    303 Walnut St., Agawam   **789-2800**

Southampton Bicycle Center
    247 College Hwy, Rte. 10, Southampton **527-9784**

Specialized Sports
    Putney Rd., Brattleboro VT   **(802) 257-1017**

State Line Cycles
    1734 Longmeadow St., Longmeadow   **567-1668**

Valley Bicycles Ltd.
    319 Main St., Amherst   **256-0880**
    8 Railroad St., Hadley   **584-4466**

Waltz Ski & Bike
    309 Conway St., Greenfield   **(800) 577-5306**

Notes

New England Cartographics
Price List

Maps

Holyoke Range State Park (Eastern Section)	$3.50
Holyoke Range/Skinner State Park (Western)	$3.50
Mt. Greylock Reservation Trail Map	$3.50
Mt. Toby Reservation Trail Map	$3.50
Mt. Tom Reservation Trail Map	$3.50
Mt. Wachusett and Leominster State Forest Trail Map	$3.50
Western Massachusetts Trail Map Pack (all 6 above)	$13.95
Quabbin Reservation Guide	$3.95
Quabbin Reservation Guide (waterproof version)	$5.95
New England Trails (general locator map)	$2.00
Grand Monadnock Trail Map	$3.50
Connecticut River Map (in Massachusetts)	$5.95

Books

Guide to the Metacomet-Monadnock Trail	$8.95
Hiking the Pioneer Valley	$10.95
Skiing the Pioneer Valley	$10.95
Bicycling the Pioneer Valley	$10.95
Hiking the Monadnock Region	$10.95
High Peaks of the Northeast	$12.95
Great Rail Trails of the Northeast	$14.95
Golfing in New England	$16.95

Please include postage/handling:

$0.75 for the first single map and $0.25 for each additional map; $1.00 for the Western Mass. Map Pack; $2.00 for the first book and $1.00 for each additional book.

Postage/Handling _____

Total Enclosed_____

Order Form

To order, call or write:
New England Cartographics
P.O. Box 9369, North Amherst MA 01059
(413) - 549-4124
FAX orders: (413) - 549-3621
Toll-Free (888) 995-6277

Circle one: *Mastercard*   *Visa*   *Amex*   *Check*

Card Number_____

Expiration Date _____

Signature_____

Telephone (optional) _____

Please send my order to:

Name _____

Address _____

_____

Town/City _____

State _____   **Zip** _____